Winning Your Rebid

How to Retain Contracts through Successful Competitive Rebids

NIGEL THACKER

Routledge
Taylor & Francis Group

LONDON AND NEW YORK

First published 2012 by Gower Publishing

2 Park Square, Milton Park, Abingdon, Oxon OX14 4RN
711 Third Avenue, New York, NY 10017, USA

Routledge is an imprint of the Taylor & Francis Group, an informa business

First issued in paperback 2016

British Library Cataloguing in Publication Data
Thacker, Nigel.
  Winning your rebid : how to retain contracts through
  successful competitive rebids.
  1. Letting of contracts. 2. Negotiation in business.
  I. Title
  658.7'23-dc22

Library of Congress Cataloging-in-Publication Data
Thacker, Nigel.
  Winning your rebid : how to retain contracts through successful
competitive rebids / by Nigel Thacker.
       p. cm.
  Includes bibliographical references and index.
  ISBN 978-1-4094-4035-2 (hbk)
  1. Contracting out. I. Title.
  HD2365.T46 2011
  658.4'058--dc23

                                                                          2011034465

ISBN 978-1-4094-4035-2 (hbk)
ISBN 978-1-138-26172-3 (pbk)

Winning Your Rebid

Contents

List of Figures   *vii*
List of Tables   *ix*
About the Author   *xi*

Introduction   1

PART I   **RUNNING THE CONTRACT TO HELP YOU
              WIN THE REBID**

1   Starting the Contract with the End in Mind   13

2   Measuring Performance   25

3   Adding Value and Continuous Improvement   45

4   Managing and Reducing Risk   57

5   Keeping the Contract Relevant   69

6   Customer Relationships   93

PART II   **PREPARING FOR AND RUNNING
              A SUCCESSFUL REBID**

7   Rebid Preparations   105

8   The Rebid Strategy   113

9   Preparing the Rebid Solution   117

10   Pulling It All Together   127

Index   *149*

List of Figures

I.1   Contracts completion   9

4.1   Factors impacting on level of risk to customer of choosing
        the wrong contractor   58

5.1   Level of capabilities potentially required by changes in
        customer needs   76

5.2   Impact and cost of potential changes required to meet
        customer needs   77

6.1   Simplified relationship map showing stakeholders' view
        of the contract and their relationships   98

List of Tables

1.1   Simplified example of a promises register   18
4.1   Overly simplified statements sometimes used
            in incumbent's bids   60
7.1   Example of a customer rebid timetable   106

About the Author

Nigel Thacker has 17 years' experience in the field of bidding and rebidding. He created and ran the Best Practice Centre in Serco PLC (a FTSE 100 company specialising in Support Services), developing techniques and processes in Bidding, Rebidding and Contract Management.

He has trained directors, managers and staff across the world in how to run and deliver successful rebids.

Nigel has held posts including Managing Director, and Business Development Director in businesses delivering software, facilities management, logistics, construction and support services and has won rebids in markets such as Education, Local Government, Health, and Housing.

Introduction

There is an ever-growing market for services, products, consulting and many other types of offering that are being contracted out to businesses, not only from the public sector across the world, but also from the private sector. Whilst a proportion of this is for one-off services or projects, much is for ongoing services or product supply where a set period of contract is let. At the end of this period the customer puts the contract back to the market to enable a competition amongst potential suppliers so that the customer gains an advantage in price, service level or type of contract provision for the next period.

Over the past decade or more the sophistication, size and length of these contracts has grown and many larger contracts can last for five, 10 or even 25 years. Whatever the length of the contract the incumbent contractor will eventually face a competitive rebid. Whilst the incumbent should have many advantages over its competitors when it comes to winning the rebid, few if any businesses retain all of their existing contracts. Whilst some may have high rates of retention, many lose a quarter, half or even more of their existing contracts when they are rebid. This rate can vary by industry and by customer, but even within the same industry contract retention rates between companies can vary dramatically.

This book aims to give businesses an insight into how they can improve their retention rate for their existing contracts. There are a number of actions an incumbent can take that will give them a significant advantage when it comes to rebid: actions taken by some of the businesses that have retention rates in the 90 per cent bracket. These actions start right at the beginning of a new contract and follow through the whole period of delivery culminating in the bidding process. If the incumbent has taken the right actions, it should be in the best possible position to beat its competitors and retain its contract.

The Benefits an Incumbent Should Have At Rebid

If the incumbent company has provided a good service during the contract period it should have a number of advantages when the rebid comes along that will increase its likelihood of retaining the contract. Many of the points made in this book are ways to maximize these benefits. So, before going into detail about any particular areas, it is worth summarizing what these benefits should be:

UNDERSTANDING THE TASK

The incumbent has been delivering the contract for the previous period of the contract – perhaps for many years. It should therefore have an in depth understanding of the tasks that the contract involves; how they are best delivered, how much it costs to deliver them, what are the risks and potential issues, what works best, what is preferred by the customer, what does not work so well, what end-users prefer and who they are. Even if competitors are delivering similar services elsewhere, the direct and specific knowledge of how to deliver this particular contract will be known in more detail by the incumbent than by competitors (in many cases the incumbent will know more of how to deliver the contract than the customer themselves).

UNDERSTANDING THE CUSTOMER

The incumbent has been working with the customer on this contract for a number of years. It should have built up a clear knowledge of the customer and built strong relationships with key individuals. This knowledge should extend beyond the individual relationships built up in day to day contacts required to run the contract, it should extend to the wider customer. The incumbent should know who is important in decision making and what they want of the contract. The customer's key drivers, aims and worries should be clearly known, and how these are best delivered or allayed. Similarly the customer should know the incumbent and know the people involved, have positive relationships with them and prefer them as people they can do business with rather than people from competitor teams they may not know.

PROOF OF DELIVERY

The incumbent should be able to prove that it has been delivering the services or products required as it should have data to do so readily available. Whether this is a history of Key Performance Indicators (KPIs) that are important to the customer and specified in the original contract, or data that the incumbent has collected itself, such as end-user satisfaction or internal data on volumes, delivery to time, budget, specification etc., this should all be uniquely available to the incumbent to use in the rebid. In addition, the incumbent should be able to show how performance has improved over the period of the contract and where it has delivered beyond the requirements of the contract to add value for the customer.

REDUCED TIME TO GET UP TO SPEED

As the incumbent is already delivering the service or product, has the people, assets, systems, offices etc., in place, it should be the provider that can deliver from day one of the new contract with no settling in period to bring these into play or get used to the requirements of the customer which may, if a new provider was delivering, mean a period of reduced service for the customer.

LOWER RISK

Because of all the above factors, the incumbent should represent a lower risk to the customer compared to taking on a different supplier. Also the incumbent should be fully aware of all the risks involved in delivering the contract, both for itself and for the customer, and have put in place actions that mitigate those risks.

COMPATIBLE CULTURE AND APPROACH

The incumbent should know the customer's culture and approach to business and have adapted its own service and delivery to fit with this. Perhaps the customer prefers significant planning to be done and documented or perhaps they require a flexible, responsive approach. The customer may be focused on particular organizational or corporate goals that filter into how the contract is run (for instance, a strong focus on the end-user, or the environment). Individual managers or departments within the customer's organization may have a particularly strong influence on how the contract is run, or what the priorities are for how work is delivered. Whilst competitors may have gathered some intelligence on all of the above, it is the incumbent who should know what they mean in detail on a practical level and be able to reflect them in their rebid proposal.

All of the above, and potentially a number of other advantages, are there for the incumbent, to use at the rebid. However they are only potential advantages.

If the incumbent has not taken the actions that make the most of these advantages during the period of the contract, or fail to make the most of them in the rebid then they are wasted and the advantage lost.

Much of this book is about how an incumbent can make the most of these advantages in the rebid and how to prepare the best way to use them. As might be becoming clear already this is not just a task left until the actual bidding period of the rebid. To make the most of these advantages the foundations need to be put in place at the very start of the contract. The following chapters cover each of these areas in more detail and takes a journey through the contract period from the start to make sure that when the rebid comes all of the material and benefits are in place to use to keep the contract.

Impact of Losing a Rebid

The flip side of retaining a contract is of course losing it. Before moving into the bulk of the book it is worth looking briefly at the wider implications of what losing a rebid might mean for the incumbent, both as a warning, but also as a checklist to think about in the event that you as the incumbent may be thinking of not rebidding the contract. Obviously there is the financial impact of losing the revenue, profit and cash that the contract (hopefully) generated, but there can be other impacts:

- The loss of a reference – this contract cannot now be used as an existing reference with potential new customers for the businesses capabilities.

- Potentially (if this was the only contract with a particular customer) the loss of a customer and the direct contact with them that might have generated further business.

- The loss of skills that may have been resident in the people delivering the contract (assuming they are not found roles elsewhere in the business).

- Potentially the loss of critical mass in a marketplace or region.

- If this was one of few contracts delivering a particular type of service, the loss could mean the company has difficulty winning more business of this particular type – effectively exiting the business from a whole area of delivery.

- The cost and effort required to demobilize the contract and hand over to the winning competitor can be significant and can drain resources from other more positive activities.

- A decrease in confidence: within the business; within those contracts due for rebid in the near future; perhaps with existing or potential customers; possibly with investors regarding the capabilities of management and the future returns from the business.

- An increase in confidence for competitors – are there other contracts that can be attacked, or are managers deflated and looking for a move out of the losing business?

Beyond the impact of the loss of an individual contract is the cost to a business of having a low retention rate across its contracts. If a business loses 50 per cent of its contract at rebid this means that it has to replace 50 per cent of its business over the period through new wins, just to stand still. With the number of new bids that require investing in at the most likely lower win rate for new bids to cover this 50 per cent loss, investing in existing contract and rebids to increase their retention rate can pay dividends. An increase from 50 per cent retention to 75 per cent retention would equate to a 25 per cent growth rate if new business investment and success were kept constant. So investment in time, effort and resources on rebids can underpin significant increases in growth, at lower cost than the same growth rate achieved just from new business.

Getting the Most From this Book

I have broken this book into two main sections. The first covers the whole period of the contract from its very start, the second focuses on the period prior to and during the rebid.

A well-run contract that delivers to or even exceeds the customer's requirements is one of the most important aspects of increasing success at rebidding. The first half of the book is aimed primarily at those who have influence over how contracts are run and delivered, for instance contract managers and directors, account managers and operation leads. It covers a range of areas that many companies will already be delivering to a greater or lesser extent, whether through the processes set up by the company for all contracts, because of the specifications set by the customer in the bid, or simply through good contract management. Each chapter focuses on how the subject covered can be made more useful and relevant to helping win the rebid and how processes can be initiated as early as possible during the contract that will put the company in the best possible position when the rebid comes around. For operational managers this will be the most relevant part of the book and will hopefully give you a range of actions to set in motion over the coming weeks or months. In some chapters I describe areas of work (such as 'Measuring Performance', in Chapter 2) where there is a rich library of books, training courses and experience in the subject. Where this is the case I have not attempted to repeat or create a full summary of the subject. In order to keep the focus on rebidding I have only briefly summarized the subject and described those elements that are relevant to making sure that you can best prepare the contract for the rebid.

The second half of the book is aimed more at those who will be directly involved with the rebid itself. This might include bidders or other members of the rebid team as well as contract managers with rebids coming up over the next year or so. It focuses on how the work in the first half of the book can be put to best use in the rebid, and the preparations, processes and actions that will help as the rebid progresses. For contract and operational managers this half of the book should also help illustrate how the actions recommended in the first half of the book will come to fruition at the rebid, and give some preparation for the often difficult and sometimes worrying period that is the rebid itself. As with a number of areas in the first half of the book I have not attempted to turn this into a book that repeats or aims to improve on the significant amount of advice, courses or books that are available on the processes, skills and techniques of bidding itself. To do so would significantly expand the size of the book and change its focus. My assumption is that if you didn't have these skills available you would not have won the contract in the first place! Whilst all of these skills will form a part of what is required in winning a rebid I have focused on the areas that either need a greater emphasis for a rebid, need to be looked at from a different perspective for the rebid, or are unique to rebidding as opposed to bidding for new business.

If you are a rebidder who is reading this book with only a few months or weeks before the rebid process starts then I suggest you go straight to Chapter 10 to review where you are in terms of your preparation for the rebid, complete the table on the level of information you have to hand, read the section titled 'Actions If You Are Not Fully Prepared' and identify from there your priorities. You should then focus on the second half of the book. If you do have time to read the first half of the book over the coming weeks then it will give you some context to the information you may want to collect for your rebid – but you may find it of more use in working with your operational colleagues to make sure your next rebid is for a contract that has been pre-prepared for the rebid through its life.

At different points in the book I have included short notes aimed at Directors (the first is on the following page). These are aimed at those who have a number of contracts within their realm of responsibility and who may want to look at instigating some of the processes described across their division or business. I would also recommend Chapter 7 for readers in this position, who do not want to go through the book in chapter order from start to finish. This covers the team structure for rebids and the timing for allocating resources to rebids to get the best start.

I have also included a number of examples of contract or rebid situations that illustrate some of the points made in different chapters. All of these are real examples. However, in order to ensure that the companies, customers or individuals involved are not identified, I have either generalized or changed certain details or circumstances of the contract or rebid. I hope however that they still give useful illustrations of what can go right (or wrong) in different situations.

I have mainly used UK examples and terminology through the book. However, experience of rebids in a number of countries across Europe, in the USA, Australia and elsewhere has shown that whilst terminology and details of procurement processes vary to a degree, the principles and processes of improving your chances of winning a rebid are generally the same. Whilst private and public sector rebids vary, with public sector processes governed by legislation and regulation and private sector procurements generally more flexible, again the principles and processes for successful rebidding apply to both.

To help 'translate' for those familiar with the terms used in different countries or regions, some of the acronyms used in places in the following chapters and their general equivalents are briefly explained below:

OJEU = Official Journal of the European Union. Term used for notices of public sector customers that they intend to procure and that interested potential suppliers should express their interest in bidding.

PQQ = Pre-qualification Questionnaire. Used mainly by Government customers in the UK and Europe as an initial stage in the procurement process to gain core information on potential suppliers and their capabilities. Customers typically use to create a shortlist of suppliers for the next stage of bidding. Equivalents will be RFQ or Request for Qualifications.

ITT = Invitation to Tender. Documentation used by customers, usually public sector, to ask detailed questions of suppliers about how they will deliver a contract and to give a price. Equivalents will be RFP (Request for Proposal) or for Government customers in the USA and elsewhere RFT (Request for Tender).

BAFO = Best and Final Offer. The final price and solution from a supplier from which the customer will choose their preferred bidder or winner of the contract.

DIRECTORS NOTE 1

Many companies have a breakdown of when their contracts will be rebid over the coming years. The format will vary, but it is a useful planning tool to ensure that you have in one place a view of all your contracts and when they expire.

Not only will having a clear breakdown of when all your contracts are due for rebid give a view that will help in planning forecasts for future years, it will also give an indication of when you need to plan for resourcing rebid teams and budgets, such as bid managers etc., who you may normally be using to win new contracts.

Make sure that you include the value of each contract in this summary. In larger businesses the summary might be broken down by sector, product/service type or even customer. When you do this analysis for the first time you may find that you have a significant proportion of existing business at risk due to rebid within a particular year, perhaps of your total business or within a particular sector, product set or customer.

Knowing this will help you to plan your response well ahead of time. Whilst your peers might not see it as a positive approach to growth, you may consider downgrading your growth forecasts in that area or year to ensure that you are managing the risk to your forecast that such a large proportion of rebids might entail. No one wants to be accused of defeatism in planning a forecast that assumes losing existing contracts, but taking a realistic look at previous rebid win rates and applying this to your forecast of future rebids at least gives you a base to work upwards from due to your efforts in retaining your contracts. You may also need to allocate extra costs and resources in your budgeting plans to address the increased rebid activity. Or you might plan for extra growth, innovation or other activities in particular markets to balance the risk of losing rebids. You may also need to look at your team balance and ensure that you are developing or recruiting the people you will need to use on your rebids well ahead of time.

Below, in Figure I.1, is a simple version of how a plan might be set out. In this example, the immediate concern is the £22 million per annum contract due to end this coming year. Depending on whether there is time, the director involved may want to negotiate with the customer to extend this contract for another two or more years as was an option given in the original contract. Years two and three then have no rebids, however year four is a crunch year, especially if the earlier contract has been successfully extended: the director's four largest

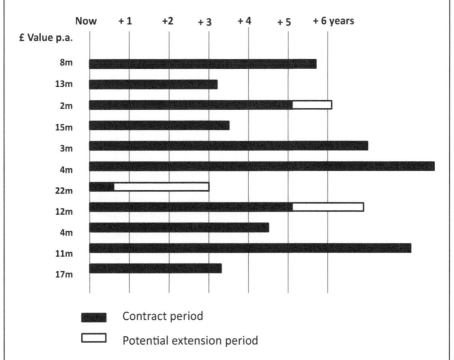

Figure I.1   Contracts completion

contracts, worth £67 million per annum of the total £111 million per annum value of all contracts are all to be rebid in that year.

Even given new contract wins in the intervening period, this is likely to be a significant risk to growth in that year, and should take up a significant proportion of the director's attention and efforts in the year – or as we will see as this book progresses, should be planned for in the years between now and then.

PART I

Running the Contract to Help You Win the Rebid

1

Starting the Contract with the End in Mind

When a new contract has been won there is a huge amount of activity in phasing in the new work, getting the staff, capabilities and assets in place, negotiations with and getting to know the customer and making sure that delivery starts effectively on day one. This process and getting to an ongoing period of equilibrium can last for the first few months of the contract and takes the attention and effort of many people in the business. Thinking about the end of the contract in three, five, ten or more years is usually the last thing on people's minds.

However this is the time when a lot of information that can be of use when the rebid does come around is available and if not captured now can be lost forever. The first few months of the contract is also the time when the business should be putting together at least an outline plan for the contract that will form the basis for how the contract will develop over its life and what it may look like when the rebid comes along.

Capturing Information

At the rebid the incumbent will want to be able to show how it has performed during the period of the contract. Usually this will mean how performance has improved over the period of the contract. We will deal in more detail with measurements and KPIs in later chapters. At the start of the contract however what the business should be looking for and capturing is the performance over the past few years of the previous incumbent, or the customer themselves if this is a first-time contract.

It should be a reasonable assumption that the contract has been awarded because the customer perceives that an external organization will deliver better outcomes than the customer can themselves. It should also be reasonable to assume that you have been chosen as the contractor because the customer believes that you will provide a better, more cost effective service or product delivery than others who bid for the work.

Capturing measures of performance of key tasks or the outputs from the contract as delivered in the previous period will, as well as giving a baseline for ongoing performance and existing customer expectations, give the incumbent at rebid what is potentially a lower baseline of previous performance that has been improved upon both at the start of the contract and ongoing. At the end of the contract period the difference in performance between pre-start and the end of the contract should show an even greater improvement than simply showing performance from the first few months of the contract to its end.

Create a Rebid File

It is worth creating a rebid file at the very start of the contract, perhaps as a standard part of the phase in or start-up procedures you may have in the business for new contracts. This may be a paper file as well as a computer file, it may be held within the contract's files or on a central business server system. Over time the wider business might set up a standardized process of including specific sub-files that are there to capture and organize specific types of information. If not, at least have somewhere to put in all early information that may be of use later even if it is not fully organized. The file and information within it can be organized later.

One issue that can be faced by incumbents at rebid is that historical information from the whole period of the contract is difficult or impossible to find. Contract Managers may have changed during the contract, the divisional structure of the business may have been realigned or the way the business collects and stores information may have changed – perhaps several times over a longer contract. Having a single place where all relevant information, that will be of use for the rebid from the whole period of the contract, is held and where information is regularly and deliberately put by those running the contract so that it is not lost, or obscured in a plethora of other files will give a source of consistent information that will be invaluable at the rebid.

Some of the information to put into the rebid file will include:

- The original bid.

- Key information from the implementation of the contract.

- Performance information (for instance copies of monthly performance reports).

- Any added value initiatives (see Chapter 3).

- Any positive customer comments or publicity about the contract.

- Updates to risk registers.

- Health and Safety or quality reviews undertaken on a regular basis.

Set-up Performance Measures

The customer is likely to have a set of KPIs against which the incumbent will be measured, there will also, of course, be a number of internal measures used by the business, such as profitability, costs, etc. The business should also look at other potential measures that can be used at the rebid to give evidence of performance during the contract. These might include end-user satisfaction, environmental impact, delivery vs. budget – whatever may be relevant to the contract. The business should also look beyond the contract itself to see where the activities of the contract may be contributing to wider customer strategies. What is the customer measured on corporately that the outcomes from the contract may be having an impact upon? Knowing these higher level measures can help the business gain other contacts with departments within the customer organization that might not be directly involved in the original contract and perhaps lead to the incumbent being seen as more than simply a deliverer of a specific service. This may be of use in developing further business during the contract period, but for our purposes the point is to create and capture a history of information across the whole period of the contract that can effectively be used at rebid. For more on measuring performance on the contract see Chapter 2.

Ask the Customer Why You Won the Contract

Many companies will review with the customer why they did not win a particular bid (and public sector organizations are in fact obliged to give some information regarding evaluation scores and will also give further feedback). However it is surprising how few companies consistently ask the customer why they won a contract.

The assumption could be that the customer was impressed by the businesses experience, capability, people, the price submitted and all of their proposals of how they would run the contract and the promises that were made in the bid. Of course, much of this will be true, otherwise a competitor would most likely have been chosen.

However, some areas may have been of more interest to the customer than others, and whilst the proposal submitted might have scored highest compared to the competition, it may not contain all the things, or aim to deliver the contract in exactly the way, that the customer really wants. Finding out what areas the customer is most interested in and what were the decisive parts of your offer in the bid process will give the incumbent a strong indication of areas to work on that will be seen as positive by the customer. Understanding any areas of weakness in the bid will also be important – not only for future bids, but as areas to focus on to show the customer you are fully capable of delivering strongly in all relevant areas.

Depending on how the customer is structured, this may also be a final time that some of the customer's management – from areas such as procurement or other senior managers who were involved in the procurement process and decision – are involved in detail in the day to day running of the ongoing contract. It will not hurt to make a final good impression with them, and to hand over an element of the relationship with them from the bid team to the ongoing operational team who have the opportunity to keep this going on a more regular basis. The next time these parts of the customer organization are deeply involved is likely to be at rebid.

Use and Keep a Promises Register

We are straying into good practice for Phase Ins/Implementation processes here, however, as always the point is to have a record for the rebid. A promises register is used by some companies to capture on a single sheet (or a few sheets) all the promises that were made to the customer during the bid process of what the business would do in the contract period. Bids can be voluminous documents spread over many sections and it is easy to forget what exactly the bid team has promised will be done (look for all the phrases starting with variations of 'we will'). The customer will have read and evaluated the document, listened to presentations and perhaps gone through phases of negotiation before awarding the contract and will have chosen the winner based on what they have said they will do on the contract for the price proposed.

Capturing all these promises and commitments in one place is used by some companies within their bid as a supplement to the executive summary. For others many of the commitments relate to the implementation process and are captured within the implementation plan. However collating all of these promises, including those that apply across the whole contract period, into a short table and sitting down with the customer at the start of the contract to review the table can help ensure that what has been promised is exactly what the customer actually wants. Remember, just because the customer chose you, they may not want everything you promised to deliver to be done the way you proposed. In some cases you may find that the customer does not want some of the initiatives you have proposed, potentially saving you money or enabling you to add to other areas that the customer sees as important that were not included in your bid or costings. You may end up negotiating with the customer around how these promises are to be delivered, but eventually the promises register should form a key part of the background documentation against which you are delivering the contract. As these promises are delivered they can be signed off by the customer. When the rebid arrives this document can form a useful tool to prove that the incumbent has indeed delivered what it originally promised and will remain a useful reminder of all the changes and improvements that were put in place earlier in the contract and through its life to be used as part of the rebid.

For a simplified example of a promises register, see Table 1.1.

Table 1.1   Simplified example of a promises register

Section in bid	Promise summary	Delivery by	Action for start up meeting
CC1	Set up procedure for orders, survey, etc.	Month 1	Agree with Customer at start up meeting
CC3	Integrate IT system	Month 3	Programme and contacts for getting integration
CC4	Vehicle reg, staff ID	Immediate	Format required by Customer– template, staff
CC7	Conduct joint inspections	Ongoing	Agree inspection process
CC10	Order and hold stock	Month 1	Agree specs, initial programme agreed
CC11	Pre-inspection forms	Month 2	Agree form template and who to do inspections initially
CC13	Route for complaints	Month1	Communicate with tenants/agree process with Customer
CC14	Booklets for customers	Month 4	Agree contents and distribution
CC14	Agree measures of client satisfaction	Month 4	Agree KPIs and how to measure
CC15	Identify vulnerable tenants	Month 1	Agree process for communication from Customer
HSE8	Sustainable sourcing, waste and recycling	Month 2	Discuss needs with Customer
HSE9	Environmental booklet for tenants	Month 4	Agree format/contents
Mgmt1	Team set-up	Immediate	Agree with Customer – set-up team – agree
Mgmt12	Invoicing procedure	Immediate	Agree – IT system to do or paper initially
Mgmt13	Reports	Month 1	Agree what Customer would like to see
PP1	Set up partnering process	Month 6	Agree with Customer what, when, who
PP4	Agree implementation process	Immediate	Times, actions, meetings, dates

Record the Implementation of the Contract

Especially if the contract is a new win for the business there will have been an intensive period between when the customer confirmed the winner and the beginning of operation of the contract where you will have been mobilizing resources to be able to start the contract effectively. Implementation of many of the changes proposed in the bid may also carry on for some time after the contract begins operation. Many businesses put in place a dedicated 'phase in' or 'implementation' team to ensure that the programme of work required deliver a successful contract start and the changes to the operations to meet the proposed solution. Once this work is complete members of this team may segue into roles on the contract, they may move onto other implementations or other bids, or return to other roles from which they were seconded to complete the mobilization and implementation programme. Programme plans, meeting notes, reviews with the customer, sign-off's by the customer of completed actions on your promises register and perhaps a final review with the customer at completion of the implementation to capture learning will all have been tools created and used during this intensive period. Don't lose them. As the incumbent, your proven ability to deliver a significant and effective implementation and programme and will be an important part of your rebid. The fact that you have delivered such a programme for your customer on this contract is something that your competitors will usually lack. Whilst they may be able to effectively point to successful implementations of large and complex contracts for other customers, you as the incumbent will be uniquely able to point to this record of directly relevant success. However, if these documents are not captured at the time then they may well be lost. By the time the rebid comes around a number of years may have passed and those on the contract, both within the incumbent contract team and in the customer team, may have forgotten the success of the phase in or implementation and no evidence to show this success may be available. Capturing key documents from the implementation period and details of a final review with the customer, hopefully with positive comments from them of its success, will give extremely useful evidence of your capabilities in delivering successful change when the rebid comes around.

The Contract Plan

Whether the contract comprises a number of discrete projects, such as with a framework contract, supply of a particular product, an ongoing service or other form of deliverable, it forms the foundation to create and build a relationship with the customer. Longer term contracts particularly have the opportunity to evolve, either through improvement in delivery, expansion into other areas or a wider transformation of the offering delivered to the customer. Many customers now expect the incumbent to be working with them through partnering arrangements, collaboration, or through a process of continuous improvement to improve delivery and reduce costs over the contract period as a standard part of contract terms.

However, as the initial period of implementation is completed and delivery has reached equilibrium, internal drives and focus within the incumbent supplier can move from this longer term view to the day to day issues of short-term delivery, and of management requirements to maintain or improve the planned profitability of the contract. This can lead to an opportunity missed to see the contract period as a chance to take the service delivered to a much higher level. Just as few businesses would allow themselves to remain static for three or five years, if they want to remain competitive, and to avoid this put in place plans to improve and change, it also makes sense at the beginning of a contract to ask where the business wants the contract to be at the end of its tenure and put in place at least an outline plan to achieve this.

The difference at rebid time between an incumbent that has delivered to the original contract specifications, but has only made marginal improvements or changes on an ad hoc basis (or as pushed by the customer), versus one that has planned and implemented a clear programme of development can be dramatic – and can have a dramatic influence on the chances of success in retaining the business through the rebid.

Putting in place a contract plann during the first few months of the contract that sets out a long-term plan for improvement and change, ensuring that there is a focus on implementation though the contract, and regularly reviewing and updating progress will ensure that significant improvement can be delivered over the contract period.

What should a contract plan include? A good starting point is to look at your business' own planning process (by this I mean the strategic planning process, not just the financial forecast) and apply the elements that you include in this to the contract. The context may be somewhat different, but the principles and key areas that you include will be similar. To keep this book focused on the rebid, rather than stray into general planning processes, we will not go into any depth on what this entails, but the following list of questions to ask yourself and your team may give an outline of the areas to include:

- What do we want the contract to look like at the end of the period?

- How can we make this contract as strong a reference as possible to help win business with the most demanding or innovative of customers?

- What are the contract customer's own strategic priorities and plans for the period and how can we fit with these?

- What are the relationships we want to develop with the customer over the period, including at what level, which departments and which individuals?

- What information do we want to have about any end-users of the contract services or products, what relationship do we want with them and what do we want them to think of us and our product or service?

- How will technology change over the contract period and how can we exploit this to improve the delivery of the contract and/or improve profitability?

- What costs can we reduce over the contract period and how much of this benefit (if any) do we want to pass onto the customer in lower prices?

- What other new innovations are relevant to our contract services or products and how will we develop the contract to include these?

- What level of service do we want to be delivering at the end of the contract vs. the start and how will we achieve this?

- What levels of skills and capabilities do we want our staff and managers to have at the end of the contract and how will we develop and use these, for instance to bring on new managers for use in succession planning within the contract or elsewhere within the business?

- What should the organization structure of the contract look like at the end of the contract period and how will we move towards this?

- What Corporate Responsibility goals might we want to achieve during the contract? How can we align these with the customer's own priorities?

- How will we measure progress of the changes and what governance structure should be put in place (e.g. customer meetings, internal meetings) in order to discuss, decide and drive the changes in the plan and ongoing development of the plan itself?

Your ideas and objectives for the end point of the contract need then to be set into timed targets over the contract period. For instance, what level of skills will have been increased over the first two years and what actions will be put in place to achieve this? By how much will customer satisfaction be targeted to be improved per year and again, what actions will be put in place each year to deliver this? Building improvements over improvements, even relatively incrementally over the years will add up to a significant change over the contract period.

Of course, all of the above need to be placed into the context of ensuring that the contract does deliver an acceptable margin and cash flow to the business. There are few if any circumstances where it would be wise to take the contract into loss as a consequence of ideas and investments in the contract plan. Just as with the business as a whole investments need to be costed and tested against the benefits they will deliver and clear commercial decisions made about each.

The other potential restriction on the contract plan may be the contract itself. This is where the contract differs from the business as a whole, as it will usually be based on a set of criteria or specifications set out in the contract documentation. However, this should not be used as an excuse for not looking at the improvements and changes that make sense and will drive the contract forward. It is surprising how flexible customers can be when a good relationship is built up with them and the benefits to them of any changes are set out clearly. Being seen to have a dynamic and forward thinking approach to the contract is in most cases what the customer is looking for in a supplier and the fact of having and working towards a contract plan will in itself usually bring the customer into a stronger relationship with the incumbent – and of course this is what you should be aiming for at rebid time.

DIRECTORS NOTE 2

It is likely that your company will have a set process for bidding and for implementing new contracts. This may simply set out the sign off procedures for various stages of the process (who needs to sign off the bid at various points in its creation, who signs off the price and commercial aspects of the bid etc.), perhaps it may also include elements of best practice developed from lessons learned in previous bids and implementations and sign off procedures to ensure that the business is happy that an implementation is complete and the contract has been properly set up.

You may wish to include the items on the checklist for this chapter into the processes that you have for implementation to ensure that they are being consistently applied and that there is a sign off for each of them to be seen to be completed as a part of both the implementation stage of the contract, and as a part of the rebid process.

As you will most likely have responsibility for a number of contracts it is also worth looking at a process or governance procedure for the creation and ongoing progressing of contract plans. These may be part of the initial bid justification process in that addressing opportunities that have growth and change potential are likely to be more attractive than those that do not.

Ongoing, you may also wish to think about who and how you will drive the contract plan forward. Who, apart from the direct contract team, should be involved in reviewing and progressing the plan, and what processes will you put in place to ensure that you know each contract's plan is being taken seriously?

Some businesses cross-pollinate knowledge and ideas by having managers from contracts working with other contract teams to bring an external view, but from someone who understands the issues of managing a contract. Others include people from the central team to bring another view, and to ensure that the central team keep close to what is happening on the contracts.

Chapter 1 Checklist:

At the start of the contract make sure you do the following:

- Set up a rebid file.

- Capture information on the previous performance of the contract deliverables.

- Create/use and keep a promises register.

- Ask the customer why you won the contract.

- Review the implementation with the customer and keep a record of key implementation documents.

- Set up performance measures.

- Create an initial contract plan.

2

Measuring Performance

As part of the bidding process customers usually expect bidders to provide proof of how they have performed in similar or relevant contracts. This can be at pre-qualification stage and/or at tender stage and can form a large part of the marks awarded during evaluation. Even if specific numbers or performance levels are not directly asked for, evaluation teams will give more credence and higher marks to bidders that can evidence any claims made of performance levels with comprehensive performance measures. As well as actual numbers, quotes from customers or end-users (preferably with the name and position or other identifier of the person giving the quote) can add positive colour and credibility to a bid.

At rebid, the incumbent should have a real advantage in this area. Amongst all the bidders the incumbent can not only show performance from similar or relevant contracts, they can show performance on the contract being bid. Any quotes of strong performance will come from the customer themselves, their colleagues, customers or end-users. This can be extremely powerful if delivered well.

However, it is surprising the number of incumbents who do not make the most of this advantage. Of course, there is the possibility that the incumbent has not performed as well as they could and are embarrassed by the performance measures they have (in this case the problem for them will go beyond not being able to quote excellent performance measures – the customer is unlikely to be well disposed to the incumbent anyway).

More often, however, the problem is that the incumbent does not include the measures because they think that the customer already knows them and so the numbers do not need to be included in the written submission. Or perhaps the incumbent bid team do not have a history of performance over the contract period available. Both are real oversights by the incumbent and are likely to reduce their chances of renewing the contract.

The first of these two possibilities is the most easily dealt with. The second forms the major part of this chapter.

Use the Information You Have

This is a short section, but an important one that applies not just to performance measures but to all the information covered in this book. Its key message is: No matter how well the incumbent knows the customer and vice versa, even if the customer evaluation team is personally close to the incumbent's team and has been deeply involved in all aspects of the contract for the past few years, and discusses contract performance on a daily basis throughout the rebid period; the incumbent bid team must never assume that they will get marks for information not explicitly included within the rebid documents.

The evaluation process of a bid (or procurement as seen from the customer perspective) is in most cases a formal process that is likely to be audited at least by senior management who are not part of the day to day running of the contract. In the public sector there is a high level of formality, rules, governance and external audit applied to the process. The customer must be able to justify the decisions made as to who has progressed from pre-qualification to shortlist, and from there to a winning bidder. This justification has to be made within the organization; to external government auditors; and sometimes to other bidders who challenge the decisions made. For these reasons the evaluation process is usually formally laid down and often overseen by outside people. This can for instance be the corporate procurement team, external procurement consultants, or for some public sector procurements, professionals from central departments who oversee or act as auditors of the process.

Therefore the bid evaluation is likely to be set and marked to very formal processes. Scoring can only be given to particular types of information and if these are not present in the document they cannot be scored – even if the evaluators know about it from their own experience. Some bid processes even require bid documents to be anonymized by the procurement team before being given to those evaluating them, so those scoring the responses do not know which bidder they are from.

No matter how familiar the incumbent is with any information regarding their knowledge of or performance on the contract or know that the customer and evaluation team are familiar with this information, it must still be explicitly included as part of the rebid document and presentations that are part of the rebid process. Contract and rebid teams should constantly challenge themselves to make sure they are not assuming knowledge by the evaluation team of the incumbent's performance or knowledge of the contract. And this challenge should be a vital part of any reviews of the rebid documentation that are made by the incumbent business. It can be taken to the point of including people from the wider business or external consultants into the review process who do not know the contract at all to challenge the response and ask what may seem to the contract or rebidding team very naive questions about the information that is or is not included in the bid.

Collating Contract Performance

This is the core of the rest of the chapter and deals with the second problem that can face an incumbent's rebid team: is there a full history of the performance of the contract to hand when the rebid document is written?

We have already mentioned setting up the contract at the start to capture early information and measures of performance. However, after three, five, ten or more years keeping an ongoing and coherent record of performance, potentially over the management of more than one leader of the contract and any number of changes in contract team or customer liaison, can be a challenge that requires forethought and discipline as well as good record keeping. At rebid time having access to this record of performance can be invaluable, even if a day by day record of performance is not going to be included as the best representation of the incumbent's performance.

What to Measure?

Any measures that are going to be used at rebid need to be:

- Relevant to the particular operations of the contract.

- Show performance of activities that are important to the customer.

- Reflect those areas of the incumbent's performance that show competence and capability in the main activities of the contract.

- Preferably show excellence in delivering the contract beyond the levels set by the customer.

The exact items that are going to be measured will vary by the type of contract and the activities involved. The customer will most likely have set up a performance measurement regime as a part of the contract agreement and of course these are going to form a core of what is measured. These can vary from very light requirements with few measures that are done on a monthly or quarterly basis, through to extremely complex and onerous regimes with many different measures that are required on a weekly or daily basis and can even form a part of the incumbents level of payment for the contract.

However, even with the most onerous of performance regimes the incumbent should look early in the contract at whether there are elements of performance which might not be included in the customer's regime. There might be other areas of performance that they want to measure themselves because they will be of use at the rebid. For instance the customer's regime may be based largely on input measures (i.e. those that measure activity levels) but not look at the outputs of these activities, or the outcomes of the work done. For example, the measurement regime may focus on working to budget, meeting time expectations for delivery and meeting of specifications set for how the work is delivered. The incumbent might also want to measure things such as how satisfied end-users are with how the work is delivered, or how the work done has allowed the customer to achieve some key corporate aim, such as achieving a Government set target or allowed them to increase their own profits.

Inputs, Outputs and Outcomes

Over the past two decades the sophistication of contracting and of customers has increased. One reflection and result of this has been the change in how performance measures have been used. The change is by no means uniform, but there has been a definite trend away from input-based measures towards output and more recently outcome measures.

What are these different types of measure?

Input measures – look at the level of effort or resource that the contractor applies to the contract in different areas. For instance, an input measure may state that the contractor will deliver a certain number of security staff for a set number of hours in particular locations, or will clean an office in a particular way at specific times and for a specified number of days per week. The contractor will be measured on the delivery of these inputs and penalized if they do not ensure that the right number of people or items turn up at the specified time to do the specified task in the specified way.

Output measures – focus on the direct result of the work that is done by the contractor in different parts of the contract. For instance rather than measuring how many cleaners are used on the contract an output measure would specify a certain level of cleanliness, as measured in a predetermined way.

Outcome measures – move further from measuring the work that is done towards the final result that the work delivers, usually for the customer, or end-user. For our cleaning example, in a hospital this might be around reduction in patient infection levels associated with lack of cleanliness.

There can be a grey area between output and outcome measures. This may depend on the specific role of the contract in the customer's overall business. Typically the more important the contract is to key business outcomes of the customer and the more influential the work delivered to these then outcome measures are able to be more closely linked to these business outcomes. If, however, the contract work is only one of the influences on these outcomes then what may be an outcome for the contract area is really one of the outputs that have a greater or lesser influence on the final outcome. End-user satisfaction can be one of the measures that sit in this grey area. Sometimes it is seen as an outcome measure for a contract in terms of end-user satisfaction with the work delivered. The end-user here could be the customer's customer, or potentially staff members of the customer. But how much of an influence on the end-user's overall satisfaction with the customer does the contract work have? And to what degree does end-user satisfaction impact on the health and prosperity of your customer?

The type of measures used by customers can have a significant influence on how the contract is managed and the ability of the incumbent to make positive changes that will reduce costs or improve the impact the contract has on the customer.

Contracts which predominantly have input measures will tend to be quite tight in how they are managed by the customer. They will tend to define clearly what the contractor has to deliver, how this should be done and what level of resources are required. There will usually be a relatively large number of measures, which will be reviewed very regularly and any deviations from the proscribed levels will be quickly identified by the customer and required to be resolved. The customer's contract management team may be closely involved in ensuring that the detail of the specified work is delivered. The customer will have decided when making their procurement what the specified levels of work will deliver in terms of outputs and they may not be measured during the contract. Because the customer has decided, often in detail, the work to be provided, the contractors who bid will have little opportunity to offer innovative and different ways to deliver the contract and are focused therefore on delivering the specified requirements as cheaply and robustly as possible. To a degree the customer has created a commodity and they will most likely choose the cheapest option.

As measures move towards being output, and particularly outcome oriented, the opportunity for the contractor to put together solutions that deliver the outputs and outcomes in different ways increase. The customer will be less focused on how the outputs and outcomes are delivered (excepting of course that they are delivered robustly etc.) and are likely to have fewer, if any, input measures. The contractor takes the risk on the amount and type of resource they apply to the contract to deliver the outputs. Solutions may involve different types of technology, different processes, and different skill sets of staff, different locations, centralized or local services or a range of other alternatives. The ability, or requirement, for the contractor to improve the levels of outcome or output delivered through the life of the contract may also increase (either in terms of volume, quality or cost).

What is the relevance of this to the rebid? There are three main impacts that these differing types of measurement regimes can have for an incumbent at rebid:

1. The level of relationship the incumbent can build with the customer.

2. The ability for the incumbent to have made improvements to the contract performance through its life.

3. The potential for change in performance regime at rebid and the contractor's ability to demonstrate their ability to deliver against these.

RELATIONSHIP WITH THE CUSTOMER

Because outputs and particularly outcomes are likely to be of greater importance to the organizational health and competitiveness of the customer as a whole they are of more strategic importance to the customer and are likely to gain significant attention from the customer's senior management. This is likely to bring the incumbent into contact with these senior managers, and in a context where the incumbent management team will be having strategic conversations with the customer on what is of most importance to them. The incumbent team will have the opportunity to make suggestions as to how they can, by changing how they work and improving the contract performance or structure, deliver strategically important benefits to the customer. The incumbent, therefore, has the opportunity to create more of a partnering type of relationship with the customer at very senior levels. This relationship – if of course it remains positive and the incumbent does deliver for the customer – can be a significant advantage as the contract progresses and the rebid approaches and is run.

ABILITY TO MAKE IMPROVEMENTS

Because input-based measures specify in detail what the contractor should deliver to the contract rather than what these inputs result in and are often detailed in what they specify, there can be limited scope for the contractor to make significant improvements to the delivery of the contract. In contrast, the potential flexibility of how outputs or outcomes are delivered can give scope for the incumbent to make changes to the type and level of resources they use to deliver them over the period of the contract. For instance, new technology can be introduced to reduce the cost of people delivering work, substantially speed up processes or improve communication. This can lead to reduced costs for the incumbent that can be taken to profit or shared with the customer in reduced prices, or it can improve the speed and quality of delivery on the contract. Having this flexibility of how the service is delivered in the background helps drive innovation (if the incumbent chooses to) that can mean that as the contract progresses the delivery of the contract moves forward in a way that is more difficult with an input-based measurement approach, putting the incumbent in a much stronger position as the rebid approaches.

POTENTIAL FOR CHANGE AT REBID

As stated at the start of this section, customers and the market are becoming more sophisticated over time in their use of performance measures and in how they contract. The rebid is the opportunity for customers to make a step change in how they organize the contract (see Chapter 5 for more on this subject). If you, as the incumbent, have been working to an input-based performance regime and the customer intends to move to an output regime, or from an output to an outcome regime for the next contract period, how prepared are you for this? Do you know what outputs your work delivers, or do you clearly understand the outcomes that are important to your customer and how you can positively contribute to these? Has the work you have delivered over the period of the contract, even if measured via inputs, actually delivered improved outputs for the customer? From the work you have delivered over the contract period does the customer believe that you are capable of improving the outputs and outcomes that are important to them? If your answer to any of these questions is either 'No' or 'I don't know' then you have lost a potential advantage at the rebid, and could be at a significant disadvantage if the customer's view of you is as a company that is focussed on inputs rather than outputs. The contract period is an opportunity for you to look closely at the next level of performance measurement (inputs to outputs, or outputs to outcomes) and find ways to show the customer that you are not just delivering to the regime they have in place at the moment, but are able to, and indeed are, delivering at the next level as well.

ACTIONS TO TAKE

The aim for the incumbent is to understand the performance regime in terms of input, output or outcome measures and then look for ways that they can set up measures that move them up the 'value chain' in how they measure their performance, how the contract is delivered to improve these measures, and how to communicate this to the customer.

The first step is to analyse the existing performance regime. What does it measure at the moment? A simple route to this is to put each of the measures set into one of the following columns:

Input-based measures	Output-based measures	Outcome-based measures

Where are most of the measures that have been set on your contract? Do you have input-, output- and outcome-based measures for the same area of work? And if so do the inputs specified enable you to deliver the output or outcome?

Once you have clarity of where the performance regime sits at the moment, the next step is to work out what the next level of measure would be in the value chain for each of the measures that you presently have in place. For instance, if you have an input measure that states that you will provide resources to deliver a particular task, then what is the result of that task that the customer may see as relevant to them? What are the outputs, and what outcomes do these outputs contribute to (even if only in a small way) to outcomes that are key to the customer's business?

This will require you to look both forward from the activities on your contract and backwards from the key strategic drivers of the customer. These might be found in their own strategies, their Annual Accounts or plans, or in conversation with the customer's management teams. The key is to understand what is important to the customer. There is limited value in spending time working on a performance measure that the customer does not value delivery of or improvement in.

The final stage is to work out ways that you could measure the higher level performance target and how you can contribute to its improvement. This may be difficult or surprisingly easy. One factor will be whether the customer already captures the data themselves. It is surprising how little data some customers collect in areas that would be very relevant to them – and if you can find a way to collect this data from the activities of your contract, and show the customer the connection between your activities and this performance you can gain a significantly higher level of contact and interest from the customer at more senior levels, and potentially improve the position of those managing or administering your contract on the customer's team.

Present measure	What does this result in?	What outcome does it contribute to?	How could we measure the contribution?

EXAMPLE

A roofing business had held a contract with a UK Local Authority to deliver reroofing of schools for four years. The main performance measures set by the customer were based on delivery of the reroofing work to the times set for each project, keeping to budgets set for each piece of work and the number of defects that required rework at the end of each project.

A new manager joining the business in middle of the contract period realised that the company had received a number of complementary letters from Head Teachers of schools that the company had reroofed over the previous years. The manager created a questionnaire for all Head Teachers that the company delivered work for, asking for their feedback on a scale of 1–10 on a number of aspects of the work delivered (having asked a sample of Heads what aspects they felt were important to them). This questionnaire was sent retrospectively to all schools where work had been done for the previous year, and was incorporated as a standard part of the process for all school work from then on. After three months enough responses had been returned for the company to analyse the results: They were pleasantly surprised to find that the Heads were very complimentary about the flexibility of the workforce working on the roofs in liaising with Heads and school staff in stopping work for short periods when noise might disturb a key part of the school day such as assembly or exams. Other areas such as consideration for the safety of the children at the schools were also marked very highly in the responses. The company presented this information to the Local Authority team managing the contract and they were also pleasantly surprised and asked for quarterly updates on Head Teacher satisfaction levels with the work. At rebid the business was able to use this information in their successful rebid.

It was only in the last year of the contract that the business also realised that, as part of the reroofing process the significant insulation they were adding to the school roofs as a standard part of their work could potentially be having an impact on reducing the school's fuel bills. On further investigation the company found on the local authority website that the customer was corporately committed to reducing its CO2 emissions by 25 per cent over the coming four years, and that schools represented 75 per cent of the authority's total emissions. The company calculated the fuel savings that its work could be giving to schools, as well as the reduction in CO2 emissions that this could represent and talked to the Climate Change team in the authority about their findings. The customer's team had not realised how the positive impact of the roofing work that was already being done would help them achieve their targets and worked closely with the company to substantiate the figures. At rebid the company was able to use these numbers as evidence of their commitment to helping the customer achieve its wider aspirations and used positive quotes on their work from the climate change team in their proposal summary. As well as broadening the company's contact base within the customer organisation it was able to show the customer that it was thinking beyond the basics of the contract and was able to differentiate itself from its competitors – again contributing to its rebid.

Benchmarking

Customers may let a number of similar contracts to different suppliers. These may be based on geographical region, be separate phases of repeated project type work or different departments in large customers, especially government customers. In the public sector for instance different customers, such as Local Authorities or NHS Trusts, will let contracts individually that are similar to those let by many other authorities across the country.

This can lead the customer to measure performance not just against contract specific areas, but be able to compare the performance of a contractor against others doing similar work for themselves or similar customers. This benchmarking has been actively encouraged for instance by the Office of Government Commerce (OGC), the central government department in the UK responsible for (amongst other things) providing policy standards and guidance on best practice in procurement for all government departments and bodies.

Incumbents should, even if the customer does not benchmark against external best practice, aim to compare their own performance against any appropriate common measures. The exact measures will depend on the type of work being conducted, and at least initially the incumbent may only wish to do this comparison privately to check the contract's performance against, others until or unless the levels being achieved are comparable or better. By rebid time however, the incumbent should aim to be in this position and be able to use these comparisons to its advantage in the rebid.

Of course many incumbents will have a number of contracts doing similar work in a particular marketplace. This creates the ideal way to benchmark the performance of each of these contracts against the others. Whilst this might only be for internal use (you would probably not want to tell your customer that your performance on their contract is not as good as for other customers) it can be used to help understand where different contracts are performing particularly well – and then understand why this is and look to spread this best practice across other contracts to improve their performance. Of course it can also identify areas of relative weakness in particular contracts and help overcome these. Another potential benefit of doing internal benchmarking can be to help align how performance is measured across contracts.

EXAMPLE

A contractor with a number of similar contracts within a marketplace decided to move from measuring them entirely separately with no comparisons between them to an internal benchmarking regime. They found that two of their contracts had customer imposed KPIs that measured time to delivery of a certain service very differently. One customer measured in actual minutes with the contractor delivering in an average of eight minutes (an improvement of 12 minutes over the previous incumbent), the second measured in the percentage of instances delivered in less than 30 minutes. The contractor was delivering to this KPI 97 per cent of the time, but had no understanding of the actual average minutes performance on this second contract. By going back to their core data they realised that the average minutes to delivery on the second contract was in fact six minutes – a significant improvement over the 40 minutes that had previously been delivered by the customer's own in house team. When this information was presented (with the appropriate evidence) to the customer they were delighted – particularly as the contract team could also show that as this service was delivered many times a month the reduction in 'idle' time spent by customer staff waiting for the service to be completed equated to over 12,000 hours per year, the equivalent of having several additional staff members employed in their core work.

Not only did this benchmarking exercise enable the contractor to measure performance of one contract vs. the other, it resulted in being able to show the customer performance data in a way that had more relevance to them, and illustrated the real benefits that the contractor was delivering.

The power of being able to move from a monthly KPI of '97 per cent delivered within 30 minutes' to '12,000 customer staff hours saved', as illustrated in the previous, example also leads to another point about performance measurement that should be looked at to strengthen the incumbent's hand at the rebid: How the incumbent looks at performance measures can often be influenced by the internal culture and priorities of the company – and this may not reveal the best way to communicate performance to the customer. The contractor in the example above had a somewhat 'compliance' based culture at management levels – the emphasis was more on meeting the performance set by the customer than looking at new ways to view that performance and potentially improve it.

EXAMPLE

Another example comes from a company that was highly focussed on financial performance of contracts. Their customers tended to set KPI regimes that, if not met, led to a financial penalty on the contractor. Because this impacted on margins the operational management in the business focused almost entirely in their internal monthly contract reviews on this aspect and measure of performance. The measures used were '£ penalties this month' and this was how the company managed the contract and internally communicated success or lack of it. However, when a bidder working on a rebid of one of the contracts needed to communicate the performance of the business across its contracts for reference purposes this was not seen as a positive way to illustrate the contract's performance. Instead the bidder simply divided the total penalty value per year by the total invoice value per year to come up with a percentage failure rate. On most contracts this was extremely small – less than 0.5 per cent. Of course a failure rate of 0.5 per cent can be communicated as a success rate of 99.5 per cent and after checking with their customers that this was a fair way of illustrating their performance it allowed the company to use their performance measures in the rebid in a more powerful way. It also incidentally helped the CEO of the business write a more motivational article in the next internal company newsletter! Over time the company started to add this way of looking at performance in their internal reviews. They did not lose focus on the financial aspects of the contract performance but were able to use a more 'balanced' set of measures.

The key point for incumbents is to look carefully at the performance measures being used on contracts and preferably look at them earlier in the contract period than when the rebid is due. Finding more relevant and powerful ways to communicate performance can be extremely useful at rebid, and having that data to hand during the period of the contract can potentially change for the better the customer's view of the contractor's performance and potentially the relationship with them. It can also help the contractor find ways to improve important aspects of the contract's performance.

The incumbent should also keep an open mind on whether performance measures can reasonably be changed over the contract period. As time progresses and the contract matures, measures that were relevant in the early period of the contract may become less useful, whilst new measures, either new ways of measuring a particular aspect of the work being delivered, or measurement of a new aspect of the contract may be beneficial in monitoring progress. Working with the customer to ensure that measures remain relevant, or looking at new measures that will help with the monitoring of the contract can help keep the measurement regime fresh and ensure that what matters is being measured. Of course care should also be taken to ensure that useful measures are not abandoned or ignored – when it gets to the rebid, having a range of changing measures over the period of the contract can make it difficult to show the progress that has been made over the contract period, so any changes should be thought through with this also in mind.

Improving Levels of Performance

Of course measuring performance is only a snapshot that tells where delivery is at the time. The true purpose of performance measurement is to help improve that delivery by showing progress against targets and the impact of new methods or ideas that have been put into action on the contract.

Whilst having a clear history of performance through the contract period is of use, having a record that shows high and improving levels of performance is a much stronger advantage. Conversely if performance has not improved or has even fallen off this will be a disadvantage if there is no clear, convincing and reasonable explanation that can be used at rebid.

Assuming that performance is improving over time, at rebid the incumbent team will be in an even stronger position if they can relate improvements in performance to the actions that led to the improvement. This gives the customer a view of the incumbent's actions over time and shows that improvements were not just random, lucky or due to some other external factor, but the planned for result of particular efforts, ingenuity, persistence and perhaps investment made by the incumbent in order to deliver an improving service to the customer. We will look at this in the next chapter.

Ideally when the rebid team looks back at the performance figures for the contract period, they will have in one place:

- All the numbers clearly set out in a consistent form both in terms of raw data but also summary analysis.

- Charts showing the cumulative measures over the whole period of the contract as well as year by year or period by period comparisons.

- Explanation of how the data was collected.

- Any presentations given to customers that show these performance indicators.

- Minutes from any regular meetings with the customer where the numbers were discussed.

- The programmes, ideas and investments that led to improvements in performance with clear timelines showing timing of impact and reasons why the input created the improvement.

- Any feedback from customers on performance including attributed customer quotes.

If this is not already collated and available the rebid team should aim to collate as much information as possible as one of their first tasks in preparation for the rebid.

Using Performance Measures in the Rebid Documents

Obviously presentation and reporting of performance measures is going to be happening throughout the contract period as a normal course of running the contract and communicating with the customer. The rebid document may be the first time, however, that the full history of the contract performance is collated for communication to the customer.

It is wise to ensure that any performance measures used in the rebid document have previously been communicated to the customer in a similar or recognizable format. Conversely it is generally unwise to use performance measures that the customer has never seen before or present figures in a way that may be radically different from that used previously within the contract. This is because it is likely that there will at least be someone from the customer contract team on the evaluation team and if any new set of figures or analysis is used you do not want to either confuse them or create some doubt in their mind that these numbers are true or do in fact genuinely relate to the contract and its actual delivery. If they doubt their voracity they may ignore them or mark them down in their scoring of the document and your effort has been wasted – or worse put you at a disadvantage when you should have been gaining extra points over your competitors.

Therefore the incumbent team should make sure that the customer is aware of the performance figures that are likely to be used in the rebid document before hand – even if this is done via a presentation at a regular meeting under the guise of showing a history of the contract performance to date, or more informally prior to the beginning of the official rebid process to check with the customer that they agree with the analysis. This way, when the figures are used in the rebid document the customer is already familiar with them and has hopefully confirmed their agreement with them and will give the marks deserved.

Example of a Possible Future in Performance Measurement of Contracts

One of the growing developments in performance measurement of contracts is the introduction of Payment by Outcomes, or Payment by Results (PbR). There have been some examples of versions being developed of PbR in Government let contracts, notably in the field of welfare to work contracts, such as the various developments following on from the Job Training Partnering Act since 1982 in the USA, the Working Nation programme begun in 1994 in Australia and more recently in the UK through the New Deal and its successors. The principles of these types of contract performance and payment regimes are presently being looked at in the UK for a wide range of contract types in different sectors, such as the criminal justice sector.

The drive with PbR contracts is to move measurement of contract performance to a few high-level policy objectives, or what are seen by government as socially important outcomes. For instance in the welfare to work examples the core measurements of the contracts are not based on the inputs, processes or resources that the contractor puts into the contract, but how many of the service users, in this case those who are unemployed, get into a job and stay in that job for a minimum period of time. The added complexity for the contractor is that an increasingly significant proportion of payments for these contracts is only being paid when these outcomes are proven to have been achieved. Payments made for delivery of the service are often less than the cost of delivering the contract. The contractor only receives full payment that covers their costs and delivers a profit if and when the outcomes are proven to have been delivered – which can be six months, a year or even longer after the service has been delivered, or begun to be delivered for the service user. If the contractor does not succeed in delivering the required level of outcome they receive outcome payments that can be significantly less than their costs of delivery, or indeed no outcome payments at all, although there is the potential for higher levels of return if outcomes exceed expectations.

The implications for contractors are significant. Not only is there the requirement to fund a proportion of the work on the contract until the outcomes are measured and paid for, but the contractor must be very confident that the work they are delivering will actually deliver the outcome that the customer requires, as the customer has passed the risk for lower than expected performance entirely to the contractor. Whilst the performance in terms of the outcomes delivered are measured independently, the contractor will need to have a very clear understanding, and measure of what works in delivering the required outcomes, and be very clear themselves that they are able to measure that the inputs and outputs of all their actions are leading to the outcome being measured – less for the benefit of communicating these measures to the customer, but to be sure that they are on track to deliver the outcomes that result in payment.

Whilst to date PbR contracts have been relatively few and only applied in a limited number of scenarios, governments are beginning to look more closely at their potential. In the UK, pilots are now in place in the criminal justice sector where the outcome paid for is a reduction in reoffending by those in prison or on community sentence, with private sector contractors and charities involved putting their costs at risk if they do not deliver reduced reoffending by those who pass through their contracts. The government has stated an ambition to put in place PbR contracts in many more areas of this sector over the coming years. If they prove successful it may only be a matter of time before they are applied to other government sectors, and potentially taken up in some form by private sector customers.

For incumbents in these sectors the urgency of ensuring they can measure the links between what they do on existing contracts and how these inputs lead to different levels of outcomes is increasing. The benefit that these incumbents have is that they have existing contracts that, even if these are being measured in more traditional ways at the moment, they have the potential to test their work against the requirements that are likely to emerge in forthcoming contract periods. When the rebid comes around the format of the contracts will change significantly. If the incumbent has put in the work around performance measurement on existing contracts they will have a significant advantage in convincing the customer that they should be chosen to deliver the work. This knowledge and proof of capability will also aid in convincing their own senior managers, shareholders and funders that the risks that will have to be taken in providing capital to fund the delivery of the contract until payment for results are forthcoming are known and acceptable.

Chapter 2 Checklist:

- Look for meaningful performance measures early in the contract that will give a benefit at rebid.

- If needed set up new performance measures over and above those required by the customer.

- Look particularly for output measures and measures of how the performance of the contract has helped the customer achieve their goals.

- Ensure that a consistent record is kept of performance measures over the period of the contract for use in the rebid.

- Keep your records of the actions that have led to any improvements in performance with the performance numbers so that the rebid team can give clear explanations of what has led to performance improvement over the contract period.

- Look to gain quotes from customers or end-users on the performance of the contract and again, keep a record of these where the rebid team can access them.

- Do not assume the customer knows of your performance on the contract and that it therefore does not need to be included in the rebid document: the customer will only award marks for what is included in this document.

- Where possible look for external benchmarks for contract performance and target against best practice.

- Make sure that the customer is already aware of any figures or analysis of performance measures that are going to be used in the rebid document to avoid any incredulity on their part when making the document.

3

Adding Value and Continuous Improvement

Customers expect incumbents to deliver the core requirements of the contract. But as discussed in the last chapter they also expect good contractors to have improved their performance over the period of the contract – the term most often used in contracts and bids for this is continuous improvement.

Added value is a broad term covering a potentially wide range of areas but in essence it means those things you can deliver, beyond the core areas of the contract or specification, that give the customer some additional benefit over and above the basics of delivering the contract.

In many cases adding value might be something extremely simple and one-off – for instance helping the customer out when they have an issue that is not directly related to the contract. One example might be of staff working on a contract helping to clean up the customer's premises after a localized flood to ensure business can continue as usual. In other cases the value added might be more long term and important to the customer, such as using a strength that you may have as a business, or some activity that you are conducting on the contract, to help the customer achieve significant targets of theirs outside the area of your contract (see for instance the example used in Chapter 2 on performance measurement). In other areas, added value might stray into continuous improvement – looking at ways that you can improve the performance of the contract over and above that contracted at no, or limited, cost to the customer – or delivering the contracted level of performance at reduced cost to the customer.

Indeed the terms added value and continuous improvement are sometimes used interchangeably by some customers and businesses. For the purposes of this chapter we will separate them as follows:

- Continuous Improvement: a permanent increase in performance or reduction in cost of the contract.

- Added Value: ad hoc or one-off benefits delivered to the customer, and any benefits delivered to the customer outside the direct performance of the contract.

Let's look at each in a little more detail.

Continuous Improvement

At the start of the contract you most likely improved performance, or reduced costs for the customer over that of the previous supplier – or the customer themselves if the activities were previously delivered in house (that's usually why the customer chooses the winner of a procurement process). However, this is likely to be forgotten by the rebid, and indeed part of the reason for the rebid is for the customer to gain another change in performance or cost.

As we mentioned in the last chapter on Performance Measurement, you as the incumbent will be in a much stronger position if you can show that you have not just made this initial improvement but have continued to reduce costs and/or improved performance throughout the contract period.

An increasing number of contracts specify that there will be continuous improvement processes throughout the contract. Others specify (or contractors offer in bids) a gain share mechanism where any savings the contractor makes in costs, or gains made through increases in volumes during the contract, are shared with the customer.

Whether or not these requirements are part of the contract, being able to show improvements over the contract period is increasingly important; both as an indication of the contractor's alignment to the customer's needs and as an indication that this continued improvement will also be delivered over the coming contract. This is something competitors will almost certainly claim in their bids – but only you as the incumbent can prove to have done so on this contract – if you have!

Continuous improvement should feature as an element in your Contract Plan (see Chapter 1) as well as the processes, culture and management mentality, used to achieve it.

There are many books, articles and courses that give a wide range of advice and techniques for improving performance in a company. Generally, they apply equally to how you can look to deliver improvement to your performance on a contract. I will not attempt to recreate this advice here – however, below are some relevant pointers for continuous improvement that could be relevant to your contract and rebid:

1. As a company you may have your own improvement processes. Applying these to the contract will make sense and enable you to draw on any expertise from elsewhere in your business to give advice on the relevant processes.

2. Continuous improvement is not just about large scale top-down processes. Those on the front-line of your contract will also have ideas of how to improve the areas in which they work. If managed and communicated with correctly, your staff can help you to find and put into practice a potentially large number of small improvements that will add up over time to significant changes.

3. Ensure that all improvements are captured and wherever possible their impact measured. Add them to monthly reports to the customer and keep a list of them in your rebid file. Review each year the total level of improvement or cost reductions you have achieved – you may wish to do a yearly update for the customer. At the rebid being able to show the improvements you have made, and how you have achieved them, will give you a real advantage in your rebid documentation. A graph of performance over the whole period of the contract can show just how much has been achieved, even if improvement in one particular year may not seem dramatic.

4. Look closely at your customer's key needs and aims. Even a small improvement in an area important to the customer can have greater value than a larger improvement in an area of less importance to the customer. For instance if end-user satisfaction is of particular importance to the customer then focus on any area of your work

that can improve this, even if it may seem peripheral to the core of your contract work.

OVERCOMING BARRIERS TO CONTINUOUS IMPROVEMENT

There may be barriers that you will face in putting a continuous improvement programme into the contract. These may be internal – for instance continuous improvement is not part of the culture of people within the contract. In this case the literature on continuous improvement deal well with the changes required to create this culture internally. However, it may be that the contract itself and potentially even those on the customer side directly managing the contract create a barrier. Whilst many contracts are now requiring continuous improvement there are still those that, often inadvertently, discourage it. Contracts that are input based, i.e. measure only the resources put into the work conducted rather than the result of that work, can work against performance improvement. This is because they do not recognize in their specifications or measurement regimes these outputs or outcomes – and so improvements in them are equally not recognized. In this case it can be easy for a contract team to work to the input-based measures and not be motivated to look for improvements beyond internal cost reductions that improve profit. Improvement in profit is of course a very good thing, but when the rebid comes and you look back at the performance that you can show the customer it will tend to focus on compliance to the requirements – not a proactive drive to help the customer improve. To begin the process of continuous improvement it may be necessary to collate your own measures of outputs and outcomes from the contract and measure these over a few months to gain a base level of performance in these areas. Then look for ways that this performance can be improved, preferably small-scale, low-cost projects to start with. Once this improvement is starting to show, open up a conversation with the customer about your wish to help them and to find ways, within the specification to start to improve performance going forward. Usually the customer will be more than happy to work with you on this and over time it may be possible to move the performance regime away from entirely input-based to at least a mix of output- and input-based measures. Make sure, however, that in your conversations and negotiations with the customer that you do not end up with measures of inputs that you must meet that make it difficult to make changes (in how you work) that will improve the outcome.

A related example can be working with the customer to reduce costs. Some contract requirements can add significant cost whilst adding little value to the customer. In some cases this can be because those writing the contract specification were not fully aware of the impact on operations once the contract was running. In other cases it may be due to changes in the customer's needs, technology or other external factor. Keeping a regular eye on these areas, rather than accepting them as inviolate, can identify areas where, if the customer is willing to change their requirements slightly, it will enable you to save costs – and pass a fair share of this reduction back to the customer. Simple examples of this may be:

- Over complicated invoicing arrangements.

- Measurement reporting requirements that add cost in collation, analysis and reporting but which do not give actionable information to the customer, or are not even used by the customer.

- Requirements around timing of delivery of products or services that add cost but do not add value to the customer, which if changed would not impact negatively on the customer but would save costs.

Finding these areas and opening up a conversation with the customer that shows the benefits of these changes should be something that is proactively done by the contract team. Again, small changes initially to show the customer that they will gain from this flexibility may be required and it can take several months, sometimes even years, to gain significant headway. The key is to understand the cost of each activity, but also the benefit of it to the customer and focusing on those areas that add cost but little or no benefit compared with lower cost alternatives. The second important factor is making sure that the customer really does see the benefit to them, and not just a benefit to you. To understand the value of different parts of the contract you may need to talk to a range of contacts within the customer organization beyond just the contract team. Handled sensitively this can bring great benefits in understanding different perspectives and priorities within the customer's organization, and can be used to identify opportunities, as well as being a useful tool when 'selling' the proposed changes.

Added Value

Added value, as we have said above can fit into two categories: those one-off events that benefit the customer, or benefits that you as the contractor can deliver the customer in areas that may sit outside the contract.

One-off Benefits

One-off benefits may seem to be a minor part of a contract, but over time the image of you as a flexible, helpful contractor and the positive relationships that can be built up as a result can make a real difference at rebid time. The type of ad hoc added value that you might be able to deliver to the customer will obviously vary with the type of contract and the circumstances that emerge over the period of the contract, and planning for the ad hoc is of course difficult.

Instead, the culture that you create on a contract is more likely to be the key to ensuring that ad hoc added value is delivered to the customer. This is not just the culture of the management team, but the culture that the management team engender across all staff on the contract. It is a willingness to be flexible and to 'go the extra mile' as the term used in many customer service text books state. Indeed many of the cultural aspects of a customer service oriented organization would deliver the sort of flexible approach that would deliver a great deal of day to day added value.

This sort of culture requires the management team to communicate clearly and regularly to front-line staff and others from the business involved in the contract that this is what the company wishes to deliver – potentially reinforced by training sessions on what is meant by customer service and added value and how it might be delivered. This must of course be complemented with clearly aligned actions from the management team that are also communicated to staff – telling staff to be flexible and fit with the needs of the customer whilst the management team are demonstrating a very different set of priorities through their own actions will not create the required culture. As with other aspects that we have covered in this book, there are many specialist books, training courses etc., that deal with customer service in detail, and we will not try to cover them here. The point to make is that if you have delivered (and can clearly demonstrate and evidence that you have delivered) positive customer satisfaction on the contract then you will be in a better position than if you have not.

The management and staff also need to be alert to opportunities that sit outside the normal working of the contract to be able to deliver one-off benefits. These might be issues or events that impact on the customer's ability to deliver their own services or products, such as bad weather, an IT failure, failure of another supplier etc. Reacting quickly to help the customer in these circumstances, in whatever way is feasible for the type of contract that you have, or the people and resources you have available, can have a big positive impact on the customer's appreciation of you as a flexible partner with the customer's best interests in mind.

Planned Added Value

This type of added value is different to the 'reactive' and one-off type, in that it aims to add to the value for the customer of having you as a company working with the customer by looking at how you can help the customer, outside of the specific tasks within your contract, to achieve their wider goals or to work more effectively or efficiently.

This may involve looking at how the activities of your work on the contract do or can (perhaps with some changes) help the customer to achieve other aims –as in the example given in Chapter 2 where the roofing contractor found that their work was helping the customer achieve their carbon reduction aims (even though this had not been seen as part of the contract role). Or it may involve using a capability of your company to help the customer to achieve an aim or requirement they face (for instance you may have marketing capability within your organization that the customer does not have, which could help them deliver a specific publicity aim they need to deliver).

Looking proactively at where you could add value for the customer will require you to keep abreast of the issues that are facing the customer, and their own strategic aims. You should also look to understand what is important to different departments within the customer – either through keeping in contact with them directly or through the relationships you have with your existing contacts. Look also at key individuals within the customer; what are the things that are important to them in terms of reducing problems, improving performance or cost effectiveness or even in terms of their personal progression. Combining your understanding of the particular needs of the customer at a corporate, departmental, local and individual level will be a good guide to areas to look at to add value that will have a real, positive and appreciated impact.

If you have a partnering-based contract with the customer this will be something that may be expected of you and would form a natural part of the contact that you have as part of the management of the contract. However, on more traditionally managed contracts you may, if you are looking at opportunities to add value, need to look beyond the normal meetings and contract management processes and proactively drive an appreciation that you are willing and able to deliver beyond the basics of the contract.

What sort of areas might you add value to? Below are a few potential examples:

- Invoicing – does the way and timing of your invoicing help the customer in their accounting processes – would any small changes from your perspective make a difference to the customer, for instance electronic delivery of invoices, perhaps timing of invoices in the month, the way invoices are set out, or the information included on them?

- Performance information – are there any aspects of what you do that, by collecting information differently, would give the customer information that they could use to help with their own reporting?

- Customer information – do you deal directly with your customer's customers – if so is there any information that you are collecting or could easily collect that would give the customer information or insight they could use elsewhere? Or are there simple benefits that you could deliver to the end-user that would be of benefit to them and help the customer gain in terms of their relationship with their customers?

- Suppliers – are you able to source services or materials that the customer could use elsewhere? If so can you do so more cheaply that they can, or could you combine your buying power to reduce costs for both of you? Could you even go so far as working with other contractors that may also have contracts with the customer to combine your buying power for the customer to reduce costs for all suppliers and pass this onto the customer?

- Corporate Social Responsibility – are there initiatives that you have in your business that the customer could work with you on? Or CSR initiatives the customer is leading that you could participate in to increase their benefit?

Whilst these examples may or may not be relevant to your contract or customer, hopefully they give some idea of the type of initiatives that you should be looking for. The key is not to have a list of potential added value and look no further than this list (although having such as list from other contracts you may have, or work you have done prior to starting the contract, to help in understanding the customer but which were not included in the contract or your solution, would be a very good start), but to constantly be looking for opportunities where you can work with the customer to understand their wider needs and see what if anything you might be able to do to help.

The Cost of Added Value

At this point it is worth covering something that may have been worrying some readers in the section above – the cost of delivering added value and its impact on the profitability of the contract. Whilst talk of flexibility, going the extra mile and adding value may fit well with the approach of some contractors or suppliers, to others it is not how they do business. Profitability on a contract may be low, either due to the levels of competition in the industry, or how the contract was bid. The management team, or the business as a whole, may focus primarily on gaining every additional opportunity for profit from changes requested by the customer on the contract – using for instance a tight regime of Change Controls. In this case talk of giving the customer something for nothing, or spending money and resources on encouraging staff to 'give away potential profit' through delivering additional services to the customer at no cost may seem to be commercially naive. It may even go against what your company senior managers, reporting schedules and criteria for successful management of the contract that you are measured against and even the received wisdom of what your business or industry sector, tell you are the ways to do things.

You may feel that you have a customer that does not appreciate attempts to add value, a measurement regime that does not recognize it, and even a customer contract administrator or manager that is too compliance oriented to wish to see you delivering anything outside of the agreed specification or processes on the contract (this can also apply sometimes to continuous improvement). Occasionally there are customers with this apparent attitude and contract monitoring teams on the customer side who are primarily focused on compliance. In fact, I have come across one contract monitor (several years ago) who was of the opinion that if a contractor was able to deliver added value then they must be making far too much margin on the contract to be able to afford to do so, and reacted very negatively to attempts to add value or improve the service. However, this was an exception then and is even more so now.

Those who raise the question about the cost vs. the value of added value do however make a relevant point. It is commercially naive to simply keep giving extra services or improved levels of performance to the customer, or to encourage your staff to be flexible and do whatever it takes to make the customer happy no matter the time or cost it takes to do so.If this drives the contract into making a loss then its positive impact on helping to retain this loss making contract is irrelevant. However, to look at added value and continuous improvement in this way misses some points:

- Added value does not have to be delivered free to the customer. As long as the value that the customer receives is greater than they could get elsewhere, there is no reason why at least the cost of the new or changed activity should not be charged to the customer – with of course their prior agreement. In fact if handled properly some added value activities could end up as extensions to the breadth of the contract.

- You should, as with any other part of your business, retain control over the costs you are expending on the contract and the profitability of the contract. Creating a culture of added value should be done within this context and not as a free for all where costs are added and profit given away without control. Ensuring that you are aware of what added value has been delivered on a monthly basis through including it (as a positive) in monthly meetings and internal reports from departments should ensure both that you have a clear and recorded view of what is being delivered and also can ensure that the costs are managed.

- As stated above, the point of adding value is that the customer sees the value, and that this adds to your chances of winning at rebid. Any added value initiatives must ensure that they are targeted at delivering things that the customer truly values – otherwise they are of no benefit. In defining 'the customer' you should look at all the main stakeholders who will have some influence on the rebid decision, either directly or indirectly.

Making the Most of Continuous Improvement and Added Value in the Rebid

The first aim at rebid time is to have your customer fully aware of the added value you have delivered and the level of improvement in performance or price that you have given them. Hopefully this will have given them a very positive view of you as a supplier and they will be inclined to want to retain you as their contractor for the next period. As well as simply delivering added value and improvements, the processes you have put in place to enable their delivery, both internal and with the customer should also be obvious to the customer – and of course something they will be confident that you will continue through to the next contract period.

COLLATE AND REPORT INFORMATION

Ideally you will have been regularly reporting the improvements you have made so that the customer's awareness has grown over the contract – and this if possible shouldn't be restricted only to the customer's direct contract manager or administrator. If possible you should find ways to make those who are likely to be involved in deciding what form the next contract will take, and who will be chosen to run it, aware of your good work through the contract period – so that they too go into their new procurement process with a positive view of you.

So as well as whatever weekly, monthly or perhaps quarterly reporting processes are standard as part of the contract, you should consider producing a yearly review of the added value you have delivered and the improved levels of performance on the contract over the year. Small gains on a monthly basis can get lost in the 'noise' of ongoing work on the contract, but the accumulated improvement levels of a year, and even more over several years, should give a much stronger illustration of the work you have done.

Taking the opportunity to conduct a yearly review, especially if this can include a meeting with the customer to go through the year, can also be an opportunity to review together whether the areas you have worked on over the year and the focus of any added value initiatives will still be the most important and relevant for the coming year. You should aim to agree with the customer which might be the areas of focus important to them over the coming year and so give you an ideal steer for what will be appreciated most – and potentially be able to get the customer also working with you in certain areas to enable you to deliver these improvements – for instance, there might be elements of the contract specification that work against what they want to achieve and you may be able to agree to relax these areas or reduce the importance of non-relevant contract measures (that you may otherwise be penalized for not achieving).

By the rebid your improvements should be well known to the customer, and charts or other illustrations of the total level of improvements and/or added value initiatives over the whole contract (ideally including the lower levels of performance before you took over – see Chapter 1) can make your case strongly in the rebid.

Chapter 3 Checklist:

- Add continuous improvement and added value into your Contract Plan at the start of the contract.

- Communicate what you mean by added value and continuous improvement to staff across the contract.

- Set up processes with the customer to decide, initiate and review continuous improvement initiatives.

- Train staff and managers in both added value and continuous improvement if required.

- Gain an early understanding of what is most important to the customer and what areas of improvement would be most important and of most value to them both corporately, at a department level and at an individual level.

- Ensure you understand the cost of any initiative before it is begun.

- Ensure costs are managed.

- Put in place processes to collate and report added value to the customer on a regular basis.

- Ensure you get feedback from the customer on added value and continuous improvement on a regular basis to validate the value to them – potentially through a yearly review.

4

Managing and Reducing Risk

Customers procure a service, product or outsourced element of their business for a range of reasons. In most cases it will be to improve performance and reduce costs. It may be that the element being sourced is not available effectively within the business, for instance a particular skill set. Whatever the reason for outsourcing, the act of procuring from an outside supplier also brings risks to the customer. In many cases the risks of the project, product or service that are inherent in its successful delivery to achieve the customer's required outcomes become in whole or part the responsibility of the external provider to reduce, overcome or in some cases bear the burden of.

At rebid, the customer will also be looking at the risk of change. A change of supplier can bring a number of potential risks to the customer:

- The new supplier may not perform the tasks as well as the existing supplier.

- There may be a steep learning curve in the early stages of the contract when performance may dip and cause problems for the customer.

- The culture of the new supplier may not be a fit with that of the customer, or the relationship with the new supplier may not gel positively.

- The new supplier may have misunderstood the brief or contract and have mispriced the contract or proposed a solution that appears attractive but is not in fact deliverable or workable.

The degree of risk that the customer perceives in choosing one particular supplier over others will vary from contract to contract, task to task and industry to industry.

Where the product or service being outsourced is simple and its delivery is not vital to the customer's own core plans or deliverables, and where there are many experienced suppliers in the market, with well-known undifferentiated offerings, then the risks will be seen as low and will play a relatively low part in their decision. In this case the main decision criteria may well be lowest price.

However if the service or product being procured is complex and/or where it's non or poor delivery presents a core issue to the customer, then they are more likely to look in detail at risks and focus more highly on areas of quality in their decision making. If there are highly differentiated solutions offered by suppliers and each has a different type of solution to the customer's task the risk of choosing the wrong solution increases. If perhaps there are fewer suppliers in the market and they or their offerings are less well known, less proven or less understood then the risks to the customer, and therefore the risk of change, increase further. See Figure 4.1 below.

Important complex task		Highest risk to customer (best for incumbent)
Simpleless important task	Lowest risk to customer (hardest for incumbent)	
	Many undifferentiated suppliers	Few, differentiated, unproven/unknown suppliers

Figure 4.1   **Factors impacting on level of risk to customer of choosing the wrong contractor**

Quite rightly the customer will seek to reduce its own risks through the procurement process, both in terms of inherent risks within the delivery of the tasks to be procured, and the risks of changing supplier.

At the extreme, customers are wary of becoming so dependent on an incumbent that they find it difficult to run an effective competition as they risk losing the core skills or capabilities that the incumbent has built up or created as part of their work on the contract. This can lead the customer to fear that they are in some form a hostage to the prices, service levels or form of delivery that is presently provided by the supplier. Customers will seek to avoid this situation wherever possible, potentially by splitting the contract into separate geographic or task contracts even when there may be potential economies of scale or process benefits to gain from a single supplier.

Before going to the rebid the customer is likely to research the marketplace and potential suppliers and can even proactively go out to attract potential bidders. In a few cases, such as with some government programmes, the customer might even actively aim to create a market of competitors able to deliver the required service. The process of procurement will also aim to reduce the customer's risks by ensuring that competitors are tested in terms of their capabilities, solution and price. The contract that will be signed will also of course aim to ensure that the supplier is committed commercially to delivering in a way that minimises risk to the customer – just as the customer did in the original bid in which the incumbent was successful. Some customers will reduce risks by creating a 'Framework of Suppliers' all of whom have qualified to deliver the service and whom the customer can split the supply of that service between.

Using Risk in the Rebid

The job for you as the incumbent at rebid is to convince the customer that you present the lowest risk solution – as well, of course, as delivering all the other benefits the customer wants.

As pointed out above, this covers two aspects: the lowest risk of change; and the lowest risk of failure in delivering the contract over the whole period.

It might seem obvious that the incumbent would present the lowest risk of change to the customer as effectively there would be no change. But this is an area that is often misused in rebid documents: It still needs to be pressed home in the rebid and explicitly stated that you present the lowest risk for the customer, but it is not enough just to say this in these simple terms; you must justify the statement with real examples of how the customer will be reducing their risks; and by doing this implying what the risks are of choosing any other supplier.

Table 4.1   Overly simplified statements sometimes used in incumbent's bids

Example statement	What the evaluator may be thinking when they read this
We have (X) years experience of delivering this service to the customer	What has been learnt in these years? What unique insights into the customer's situation or needs have been presented in the rebid document as a result of this? How has this experience informed the solution presented – what examples are shown in the rebid document? What will it mean in terms of delivering better and more robust performance than the competition over the coming period?
Our staff are highly experienced in delivering to the customer	Will these staff be used in the coming period? How has their experience increased their performance for the customer over other staff? What does this experience mean in terms of benefits for the customer in an improved performance? Won't the staff be transferred under TUPE to whoever wins so that this experience will be used by whichever competitor wins?
We understand the customer's needs	Have these needs been explained in the rebid document more clearly than the competitors? What has the incumbent done to meet these needs? How does the solution presented cater for these needs over the coming period better than the competition does?
Our solution has been successfully delivered for (X) years	Show me how – where are the numbers or examples in the document that convince me? Convince me how this success will continue to be delivered over the coming period. Surely the solution has developed and improved over the past (X) years – tell me how and to what effect? But how will this solution meet the needs the customer has over the coming (X) years?

The example statements in Table 4.1 are generalizations of the type of words that are sometimes used by incumbents but which are really too simplistic:

Lowest Risk of Change

As the incumbent you need to be clear of exactly what risks there are to the customer of change and what the potential impact of these risks are. At the same time you need to be very clear and specific about what part of your solution will mitigate this risk based on your capabilities, experience and the detail of the solution you are presenting.

Think about what you already have in place that will help you to deliver the service better on day one of the contract with more certainty than a new supplier, for instance:

- What IT systems do you already have in place – and better, how are they embedded or connected to the customer and their operations or processes?

- Are any of your IT systems proprietary (i.e. did you develop or modify them to fit the customer's needs) that would have to be developed or customized by a new supplier – how long would this take and what might go wrong (and how much might it cost)?

- What processes and systems do you have that are similarly aligned to the customer's processes?

- Do you have existing warehousing, offices, equipment, stocks etc., that are already being used and would take time for a new supplier to set up (and invest in)?

- Are particular parts of the service being delivered by a central department outside of the contract (for instance by a shared service centre) that a competitor would need to create or deliver themselves?

- Do you have particular staff or managers with important experience or skills who would not transfer to another supplier and who it would be difficult to quickly recruit/train replacements for?

- What customer specific training have your staff undertaken (or clearances that are required) in order to work with the customer that a new supplier would need to undertake before being able to deliver the service?

- Do you have a database of some type of customer information (or information about their customer/end-user) that a new supplier would have to create from scratch? (Be careful here about who owns this information – you or the customer – and does the customer expect you to turn over this information if you lose the contract?)

- Think about the timing of a potential handover – is it at a particularly busy or sensitive time in the customer's calendar, or just prior to a key customer event – and what might be the impact of a change in supplier at this time? (Be aware though that the customer will probably have thought of this, unless the rebid timing is forced upon them, and will have put in place some mitigating actions.)

- Are there any projects or programmes that overlap the end of the existing contract period and the new contract period – how would a new supplier take these on part way through?

There will undoubtedly be other details that you will think of that will be specific to the contract. It is worth looking back at your own original phase in/ implementation of the contract and reviewing any difficulties that were faced – would these also be faced by a new supplier?

At this point there are two warnings that you need to beware of in using the above:

1. All of the above points assume that they will be as relevant to the new contract period as they are to the existing one. If the customer is changing the type or terms of the contract and the solution that they are expecting, or indeed you are changing the solution you are putting forward (see Chapter 5. 'Keeping the Contract Relevant') then some or perhaps many of the things you are presently delivering will need to change. Don't fall into the trap of either not delivering the changes the customer expects, even if this might reduce your advantages in some of the areas above. Particularly don't propose a range of changes, then forget about them in the areas of your rebid that deal with risk and imply that you represent the lowest risk as nothing will change (it can happen when different sections are being written by different people and there is no final review of the consistency of the whole rebid document).

2. Don't rely too heavily in your rebid on the risks of change to the customer; the customer will most probably have thought hard about the potential risks of change and looked at how to mitigate

them – whilst there are some contracts where the risk of change is an overriding danger that the customer recognizes they are relatively rare.

Your competitors will be also writing as convincingly as possible in their bids about how they will be able to deliver from the start of the contract. Use the points you have to make subtly as you put forward your solution: one area may be in the mobilization plan for the new contract showing how you already have many of the resources in place to deliver and giving clear targets for day one delivery. But it will usually be better to add the benefits you bring in being able to deliver from day one as you cover different parts of your solution rather than have a separate section or heading that bluntly puts all of the points and dangers to the customer of change in one place – the customer might take this negatively – they are after all your customer, not your hostage.

The points you make about the risks of change should put a small doubt in the customer's mind about the benefits of your competitor's solutions that can potentially tip the balance in your favour – but only as a part of a strong overall offering that you are putting forward. If you find that you are relying on this area as your main reason for the customer to stay with you, look again at your solution – it needs more work.

Lowest Risk to Contract Delivery

Risk registers are an integral part of most business management and planning tools. A simple risk register will list the potential risks together with their likelihood, their potential impact, who is responsible for the risk and any mitigating actions that are to be taken to reduce either or both the likelihood or impact of the risk occurring, such as in the simple table below:

Risk	Likelihood: High, medium or low	Impact: High, medium or low	Owner	Mitigation

Your risk register may also include other columns such as:

- The proximity of the risk in time (for instance if there is an event occurring in the future that carries a certain set of risks to the contract).

- Mitigation actions can be split to cover actions that reduce the likelihood of the risk occurring, and actions that mitigate the impact of the risk if it does occur.

- The 'residual' likelihood and impact of the risk after the mitigating actions have been taken.

- A red, amber and green column indicating the direction of travel regarding the risk – is it reducing over time since the last review, or increasing?

It is likely that you will have needed to prepare two risk registers as part of the original contract bid: one internal to your business (if this is included in your bid processes) looking at the risks to your company of bidding and running the contract; the other looking at the risks relevant to the successful delivery to the customer of the contract. The customer will undoubtedly have created their own risk register for the procurement and outsourcing of the contract. Sometimes this, or part of it, is included in bid documentation with the bidders invited to comment on it, add to it or show how they would reduce or mitigate the risks shown.

At the start of the contract the customer may also have worked with you to develop a shared risk register and perhaps asked you to prepare a Business Continuity Plan showing how you would continue to deliver the contract in the event of minor or major disasters, such as fire, bad weather, a major Health and Safety incident, loss of IT services, loss of key staff, a strike, etc.

For some contracts this risk register will continue to be regularly reviewed and updated throughout the contract. For some it will be 'put in a draw' and left, or updated as part of a purely bureaucratic exercise on a yearly basis or when Health and Safety or Quality Accreditation audits are due.

When it comes to the rebid, if you have treated the risk register as a purely bureaucratic exercise then you have potentially increased your own risk – of not winning. As the incumbent you should have built up a unique insight to the risks inherent in the contract and its delivery, not only from your own company perspective (in terms of cost, performance, cash flow and profitability) but also crucially in terms of reducing the risk to the customer of poor or inconsistent delivery or achievement of their goals that the contract contributes to.

No competitor, even if they deliver a similar service elsewhere, should know in as much detail as you the specifics of what the risks are with the contract. Similarly no competitor should be able to show how these risks have been addressed, overcome and reduced for the future. As the incumbent you should have a significant stock of insight, experience and actions taken that you can use to good effect in the rebid to show how you have done just this. And by implication (at least) how you will be able to do so better than anyone else for the forthcoming contract period.

The risk register is how you can collate these risks and show how you are acting through the contract to mitigate them. Far from being seen as a bureaucratic requirement it should be constantly added to and refined during the contract so that when the rebid comes it is a key source of useful and detailed information. When any issues or problems arise on the contract, these should be added to the risk register (whether they were anticipated or not, there will have been a previous risk that they might happen), together with the action that was taken to solve the problem and what has been put in place to prevent or reduce the risk of the issue occurring again and what to do if it does happen.

This can be collated as an event log, which may for instance have the following headings:

Event	Impact	Frequency	Mitigation/ preventative action	Post mitigation impact/ frequency

Creating and retaining an event log of issues that have arisen on the contract (i.e. risks that have crystallized into events) may already form a part of existing contract quality systems – for instance, a non-conformance element of an ISO9001 quality process. These events may be relatively minor and have relatively high frequency depending on the contract (e.g. a low score for service by an end-user in a contract where a high volume of end-users are served and surveyed, a near miss, a particularly high period of demand, etc.), or they may be more severe one-off or very infrequent events (e.g. bad weather closing down the customer's facilities). Whatever the event, its impact or frequency it should be standard practice to review its causes after the event and anticipate and action plans, either to prevent its reoccurrence (or reduce its frequency) and to reduce the impact if it does occur again.

Having a clear and comprehensive history of these types of events, together with the measures of how preventative actions have reduced the subsequent frequency and/or impact of them over the period of the contract will (in addition to the benefit of the likely improvement in performance seen on the contract over time) be an extremely useful source of information at rebid.

It will have the potential to help you show a clear understanding of the risks and detailed running of the contract which will add depth and credibility to the rebid. It should also help to identify risks that have been overcome/ reduced during the course of the contract that other bidders may not be aware of and so have not accounted for in their bids. It may also give real examples of where the actions and planning on the part of the contract team have delivered improvements to the running and outcomes of the contract and demonstrably reduced risks for the customer.

Identifying them within the rebid will reinforce with the customer your knowledge of the contract and how you have a solution that fits closely with the specifics of delivering the contract robustly, and with reduced risk going forward. Ideally you should start the risk register at the start of the original phase in to the contract – this will then capture the issues that were faced then and can be used to inform the risk of change list covered above.

Over a period of years this will build into a fairly long list – but it is worth having. The alternative is likely to be that a lot of the details are forgotten over time, or lost with changes in management or staff, and the information won't be available to use at the rebid.

As with the areas covered in other chapters, it is worth making sure that you are reviewing these details with the customer regularly during the contract period, rather than introducing them for the first time in the rebid. This regular contact will build the customer's confidence that you are being proactive during the contract, so that when they see the details in the rebid they can confirm to themselves that the details are accurate.

Chapter 4 Checklist:

- Start a risk register at the beginning of the contract and keep it as a live document.

- Add any issues or problems faced during the contract to the register together with how they were resolved and what was put in place to prevent or reduce the impact of them happening again using an events log.

- Review the risk register regularly with the customer.

- Create a list of potential benefits that you will bring the customer that will mean choosing you reduces the risk of non-performance early in the new contract.

- Use detail to show you know the contract and by doing so highlighting that competitors and their solutions may not cover these risks.

- Use risks of change carefully and subtly, putting them in the context of the benefits you bring – not explicitly saying how a competitor will not deliver.

5

Keeping the Contract Relevant

Even with requirements to deliver continuous improvement throughout the contract and the potential to make changes during its life, the restrictions of a contract specification or format can mean that over time it gets out of synch with the changing requirements of the customer. Even with provision in the contract to add change controls or variations to accommodate changes made, the contract in many circumstances will be out of date compared to latest market best practices and customer needs after a few years. This, together with the customer's wish to ensure that they continue to receive services that are of the best value available is why contracts are of set periods and are regularly put back to market competition at rebid.

At the same time there is potential for the incumbent to be focused on the details of delivering the contract and internally ensuring that it achieves projected cash, profit and turnover forecasts for the company. This is of course exactly what the business should be doing to ensure its ongoing commercial success. However, it should also be looking towards the rebid to ensure that this commercial success will continue over the longer term.

The danger for the incumbent at rebid time is that the contract no longer fits the needs of the customer, and the incumbent and their price or delivery is no longer in synch with the best in the marketplace. Whether this is factually true or is the perception of the customer, it can be a problem for the incumbent in retaining the contract. The benefits they would normally have of experience of the contract, positive relationships with the customer and being seen as a low risk option compared to potential competitors could be negated by the perception that the customer needs something different over the coming contract period. Even if the incumbent is delivering the existing contract well this is not what will be needed in the future. The additional danger for the incumbent in this circumstance is also that it is stereotyped by the customer as only being capable of delivering the 'old' contract whilst other businesses with other contracts more in tune with future perceived customer needs are seen as more 'innovative' or able to bring the new skills, approaches or ways of working required to update the contract.

This chapter therefore deals with two areas:

1.   Helping the incumbent avoid the risks of losing touch with the customer's changing needs that may mean significant and perhaps unexpected changes to the contract form at rebid.

2.   Helping to avoid losing touch with best practice in the market during the contract period in terms of their delivery.

The Customer's Changing Needs

As we all know, nothing stays the same for long in the marketplace or in organizations. Changes can be slow, rapid or even immediate, such as with changes in legislation. However, this dynamism is somewhat excluded from a contract due to its form being set by the contract specification, the details of its agreement and often the prices set for the provision of contract services. Even if there are a number of ongoing changes set within the contract, such as reducing prices over time, continuous improvement in delivery etc., the basic form of the contract is set for its duration. But of course the customer and its situation is likely to change over the contract period – and the longer the contract the more changes are likely to take place. So when the customer looks at the next period of the contract after the rebid, this is a chance to catch up with all these changes, and to anticipate the potential changes that are likely to happen over the coming contract period. For a five-year contract this can mean the customer attempting to make up to ten year's worth of change in one go. This can in some cases lead to radical changes to the contract at rebid that the incumbent needs to be able to anticipate and prepare to convincingly address in their rebid.

Whilst there are any number of things that can radically change a contract, below are some of the more common possibilities:

•   A change in geography over which the contract is being delivered. This may be a split of the existing contract area into smaller areas with separate contracts, or more likely in areas of growing economies of scale and consolidation in customer and supplier marketplaces, an increase in the coverage of the contract to take in new regions in the country or potentially becoming international.

- A change in the number of tasks delivered under the contract. Again this could be a split in the existing contract task packages into separate contracts (perhaps combined with a spread in geographical delivery for each) or more likely an increase in the number of tasks included in the contract. This might mean the consolidation of a number of contracts supplying different tasks for the customer into a single contract.

- Change in investment required by the supplier. The customer may require the supplier to deliver capital investment into the contract to update the assets involved. For instance, the contract may change from a simple supply of services to a Private Finance Initiative (PFI) type contract.

- A move to outcome measures. The customer may move from simply expecting the supplier to deliver the service or product to a set of input specifications, to asking bidders to deliver customer strategic outcomes. Don't be fooled into thinking this is simply a change in the performance measurement regime of the contract. It can mean a profound change in the expectation the customer has of what is to be delivered, the understanding and capabilities expected of the supplier in delivering these outcomes and how the contract is organized. For instance, it may mean that the customer expects the supplier to deliver directly to the customer's own customers or end-users. This could entail ensuring that the end-user is highly satisfied with the service delivered and a requirement to increase the number or spend on end-users, or even that the supplier's income will partly or substantially come directly or indirectly from payments made by the end-user base.

- New technology. This may not be directly specified by the customer but may be an area where the impact of new technology has a dramatic impact on how the contract is delivered, the organization of the contract and the investment and experience of using the technology involved that is expected of the supplier. Perhaps the customer has invested in new technology themselves, which has a major impact on their own processes in how the service is delivered and expects the supplier to be able to integrate with this technology and the new processes involved. Or perhaps new technology means that the way the contract can be delivered is changing radically by replacing people with systems, changing the locations from which services can be delivered, or the speed with which services or products can be delivered. These changes could mean that the incumbent's cost structure or way of delivering the contract may be out of synch with what can be achieved, that competitors with new technology or even businesses from other industries already working in the way expected can now offer an attractive solution. If so the incumbents experience of delivering the contract in the 'old' way may become a hindrance rather than a benefit at the rebid unless they can substantially change to meet the new expectations and market conditions that new technology is bringing.

There are two further possibilities that would have an even more radical impact on the contract that must also be taken into account in looking forward:

1. The customer may see no further need for the services delivered and may end the contract.

2. The customer may decide to take the delivery of the contract 'in house' rather than outsourcing it to a third party.

In these cases there is obviously less that can be done by the incumbent. However the actions that follow can at least help to anticipate and understand the customer's reasoning for taking such radical measures and perhaps negate them to some extent.

Anticipating and Acting On Changes in the Customer's Needs

Whilst the changes at rebid can be radical, it is unlikely that the customer will not be aware of or planning for them for some time before the rebid period. One of the activities the incumbent should be planning, therefore, is to use the contacts and relationships built up with the customer to ask them about what the customer is looking for. However, this should not be the only route to anticipate changes. The incumbent should be looking at the wider industry and marketplace and anticipating what will emerge. In order to reduce any negative impact changes may have, and if possible turn them into an advantage, the incumbent needs to look at three areas:

- Anticipating potential changes.

- Gaining capabilities to deliver in the ways that will be required in the new contract.

- Using the contract period to demonstrate these capabilities to the customer.

ANTICIPATING POTENTIAL CHANGES

The worst case scenario for the incumbent is finding out about potentially radical changes to the next period of the contract by reading about them in the customer's invitation to tender (ITT) or pre-qualification questionnaire (PQQ) when it is published to the market. This means that all the potential competitors who will be bidding for the new contract have the same time to react as the incumbent and any advantage the incumbent may have is lost. This may seem an obvious point – but it does happen.

The true benefit for the incumbent comes when it can successfully anticipate, well ahead of the rebid, likely changes that will be included in the new contract and have time to react to these and so put itself in a stronger position.

With the examples of potential changes given above, it is likely that the actions required to meet these changes will involve work outside the normal activities of the contract, potentially across the whole business, and may require investment by the business in gaining the capabilities required. Therefore the work to anticipate changes to customer needs is best not left to ad hoc thoughts and ideas that remain within the heads of managers on the contract alone. It will be best for the business to put in place a formal process that regularly reviews the contract and changes that might be relevant to the rebid. This might be a yearly meeting, which can be incorporated into normal planning processes to ensure that the thinking and actions required are captured but does not impose additional bureaucratic burden on the contract – there are usually enough meetings going on for most managers. Whether a separate meeting is held or an agenda point added to existing meetings, the key is to openly look at what changes are happening in the customer's organization and their marketplace or sector, and to capture what is happening in the supplier market (i.e. the incumbent's competitors) to see what is changing and what impact this might have on the rebid.

You may choose to use a format such as asking questions under headings used in strategic planning, such as:

- Political.

- Economic.

- Social.

- Technological.

- Legal.

- Environmental.

Or you may choose to look more specifically at the customer and contract with questions such as:

- What are the customer's future priorities? Perhaps the customer's annual accounts or planning documents are available to give some guidance, as well as asking the customer contacts that have been built up.

- What is happening with the customer organization? If the customer is merging or partnering with other organizations this may mean that geographical areas are broadening.

- What pressures are the customer facing? Is the customer growing, are pressures to cut costs becoming a priority, are end-user needs and expectations changing?

- What is changing within the customer's structure? Are departments changing or merging, is there a new leader at the helm, what changes might this herald?

- What are other similar organizations to the customer doing and what is happening more widely in the customer's sector? Even if the customer is not yet facing particular pressures or changes, are there other leading organizations in the customer sector that are making changes that the customer may choose to or be forced to make in the future?

- What are our own competitors doing? Are new ways of delivering contracts being tried successfully by your competitors and how might they be gaining an advantage from these?

- What similar types of contracts are being let at the moment and what do these look like? It may be that your own organization is bidding for similar contracts to the one presently held at the moment – what is being asked for in these contracts that is different to how the present contract is structured?

- What new technology is coming into the marketplace and what impact is this having on contract delivery? Looking at industry magazines and websites (both those read by supplier and customer sectors) for stories and adverts may give some indications beyond your own direct experience.

It is also important to look at the changing needs of end-users served by the contract – especially if these are the customer's own customers. If the contract brings you as the incumbent into regular contact with end-users, and particularly if you are directly serving the end-user through the contract, building an understanding of how these end-users needs and expectations are themselves changing will give you a direct line to an area of vital importance to the customer. Being able to understand, analyse and react to meet changing end-user needs gives you a very strong story to show the customer at the rebid. It may even be that you are able to give the customer information through your own understanding built up through the contact you have with their end-users that they do not have themselves. Sharing this with the customer can give you a place of potentially strategic importance to the customer's success.

Once a picture of potential changes has been outlined this, of course, needs to be tested with the customer to ensure that it is accurate. Initially this should be done without raising expectations of the incumbent making drastic changes that may not be possible or commercially viable within the context of the contract.

GAINING CAPABILITIES

Once a picture of potential changes to the customer's needs have been identified, the incumbent should look at how it might be able to deliver to meet these changes.

For instance, if the geography of the contract delivery is likely to be extended at rebid, can the incumbent show its capability to deliver over a wider area, or perhaps it may need to partner with another organization which is based in those geographical areas not presently covered, or build this coverage itself, or perhaps look to acquire a business that has this coverage.

Similarly, if the capabilities required are likely to be extended to include capabilities not presently required within the contract, does the incumbent have these capabilities, can it build or acquire them or does it need to partner?

The matrix (Figure 5.1) gives an outline of the areas which the changes identified may fall into. The business should look at the required change and place each into the appropriate box to help with decision making.

Business wide	Capabilities that will require changes that sit outside the single contract and may apply to multiple contracts, which the business has the capabilities to deliver.	Capabilities that will require business wide changes, where the business does not have the capabilities at the moment.
	Requires business wide strategic review on commercial cost to deliver.	Requires strategic business decision on whether and how to gain these capabilities.
Contract specific	Capabilities that the business has that require changes just to the specific contract.	Capabilities that the business does not have which are only required on this contract.
	Requires cost/benefit analysis of if and when to add to the contract delivery.	Requires decision on whether the cost is justified by the returns on this contract and the potential to keep the contract if investment is made.
	Within existing capabilities	**Outside existing capabilities**

Figure 5.1   **Level of capabilities potentially required by changes in customer needs**

High cost or difficulty		Lowest priority. Keep in mind to see if a lower cost way of achieving can be found, or to see if the importance to the customer increases towards the rebid date.
Low cost or difficulty	High priority – likely to be the first to look at and put into place on the contract or within the business.	
	High impact on customer perception	**Low impact on customer perception**

Figure 5.2   **Impact and cost of potential changes required to meet customer needs**

Within each of the boxes of Figure 5.1 the capabilities can also be further broken down to gain a view on their relative impact and cost, see Figure 5.2.

DEMONSTRATING THE CAPABILITIES REQUIRED

With the above analysis, the incumbent should be in a position to decide which capabilities it can and wishes to gain and put into play on the contract to meet the customer's changing needs. The decision of whether and how much to invest in making these changes will depend on the business and the value of the contract. However, there is a benefit to the incumbent in being able to demonstrate these capabilities during the period of the contract. If the incumbent does not show the customer it's capabilities until it is talking about them in the rebid document, the customer may not be convinced that the incumbent can truly deliver them and it has put itself on a level with those competitors who are also claiming these capabilities at the same time. In fact the incumbent may be at a disadvantage because the customer may have come to a conclusion about the incumbent based on their delivery of the contract that does not take into account the wider or newer capabilities that wider incumbent business may have. The customer may even ask why, if the incumbent has the capabilities, they chose not to help the customer during the contract period by using these capabilities to improve the contract delivery in line with the customer's needs?

Some capabilities may not be viable to include into the contract delivery during the period of the existing contract. In this case, if the incumbent business does have these capabilities elsewhere it should aim to show them to the customer during the period of the contract, perhaps through joint visits with the customer to sites where the capabilities are in use. Not only will this give the customer the positive sense by rebid time that the incumbent would be capable of delivering these capabilities, it may be possible to work with the customer to more clearly define the benefits the capabilities could bring and help them in their thinking and planning for their introduction in the future.

Those capabilities that are viable to introduce during the contract period should be discussed as options with the customer. The commercial viability of adding additional areas to the contract or changing to new ways of delivery are an obvious concern for the incumbent. However, the customer, if they do value the changes, is quite likely to work with the incumbent to find ways of reducing costs, of perhaps sharing investment and/or of paying additional fees for the changed services where they have the ability to do so. These changes may therefore be used to increase the size and value of the contract to the incumbent.

The benefit for the incumbent is of course that the customer sees them as a progressive and proactive partner, and sees the contract as continuing to be relevant to their changing needs. This should mean that the incumbent is seen positively at rebid time. It may even mean the difference between the customer extending the life of the existing contract or, if they have the ability (usually in the private sector rather than the public sector) deciding to forego the rebid and continue the contract ongoing.

The key here is time. By reviewing potential changes to customer needs regularly throughout the contract the incumbent gives itself time to acquire these capabilities ready for the rebid, or to work with the customer through the contract period to put in place changes that meet these needs. If this exercise is not done during the contract period, at rebid time the incumbent is in the same position as its competitors in attempting to gain the capabilities required.

Keeping in Touch With Market Best Practice

Even if the customer's perceived needs do not substantially change over a period, it is likely that there will be some improvements made on the supplier side in the market, or potentially within the contract. More widely this may mean new techniques or technology for delivery, or reductions in the cost of delivering the service or product. Even if the incumbent does not wish to, or cannot because of the restrictions of the contract, introduce these changes into the contract during the existing period, it is likely that at rebid time competitors will be putting together bids and solutions that include these improvements. This is likely to make them more attractive and/or significantly cheaper than the present delivery of the contract by the incumbent.

Perhaps the incumbent has introduced some new techniques or technology into their internal operations. Or, has taken advantage of reduced costs, and decided not to pass these savings onto the customer but take them as increased profit from the contract. As with other areas that have been discussed, this is a commercial decision that the business should take, based on its own situation, needs and preferences.

However, if the incumbent does introduce the changes only as part of the rebid, without having introduced them either in practice or principle to the customer beforehand, then the dangers mentioned above might be faced again: The customer may not believe the incumbent capable of the improvements based on previous experience, or might question why the incumbent did not deliver these benefits before, and so question their commitment to partnering, continuous improvement, etc.

From the perspective of a successful rebid, the best course of action is for the incumbent to keep abreast of the latest industry best practice and where possible introduce the customer to these ideas as they would for the changes in customer needs detailed above. Where feasible they may be introduced into the contract delivery during the contract, where not then giving the customer an insight into how the incumbent is using these best practices to benefit other customers.

This will again give the customer the view that the incumbent is proactive as well as willing and where possible able to deliver these to the customer, if not as part of the existing contract, then for the period to come after the rebid.

Building a Partnership With the Customer

Partnering contracts with customers are an increasing trend that can help deliver significant benefits to the customer over the period of the contract and indeed can help the incumbent in many ways at the rebid. However misuse of the term partnering (in bids and in rebids) is perhaps a trend that is increasing significantly faster than the reality. Partnering on a contract will usually have at least the following main elements:

- It will have involved regular formally organized meetings that focus on planning and introducing changes to the contract that deliver real benefits.

- It will have involved flexibility and a proactive approach on the part of both the customer and the contractor.

- It will have involved an open sharing of priorities between the customer and contractor and developed shared goals for the contract between the two.

- It may have meant that a wider set of stakeholders, such as other suppliers and the contract or customer's end-users, have been regularly involved in the meetings and discussions held.

- It will have delivered, by the end of the contract, significant improvements to the contract and ensured that the contract has remained more relevant to the customer's needs as they have changed over the contract period.

A good relationship at a business and a personal level between customer and contractor will be both a requirement of successful partnering and a result of the above elements of partnering. But without the above elements good relationships alone, whilst very useful, are not what can properly be called a partnering contract.

This may seem to be a somewhat pedantic distinction to make. Certainly there are many contracts where good relationships are built up and this can lead to ad hoc flexibility on the part of both customer and contractor and result in a number of positive changes over the contract period. Equally there are contracts where regular meetings are held that are called partnering meetings, but where a lack of positive relationships, shared goals or flexibility on one or both sides frustrate or dampen proactive and significant change or improvements being delivered on the contract. It is the combination of a proactive approach and positive relationship combined with a clear mechanism in place to make the most of this and help drive forward improvements and changes to the contract delivery that tend to be what creates an ongoing and effective partnership contract.

If the contract has these mechanisms in place already, then the incumbent should make the most of them by taking a positive approach to working with the customer (and potentially others that might attend the partnership meetings), working together to agree what is important to the customer over the period of the contract, and being open about what is important to the incumbent. Then the partners can work together to set aims for the contract, plan how these aims will be achieved, work together to deliver them with flexibility on both sides.

An effective partnership can help deliver many of the aspects that are covered in the different chapters in part one of this book:

- It helps build strong relationships with the customer.

- It positively enables a culture of continuous improvement and the flexibility to deliver this.

- Through looking at the contract in a longer term way it can fit with the contract plan the incumbent has for the contract.

- Through looking at areas to improve it focuses on performance measurement in a positive way and can enable flexibility in bringing in relevant measures.

- It can help keep the contract relevant to changes in customer needs.

By the end of the contract there should for the rebid be a strong record of achievements to be able to reference in the rebid, and the proven success of the partnering approach itself can be a powerful message, given with plenty of evidence, that the incumbent is the best provider for the next contract.

An Example of a Changing Market

To give a sense of how markets can change, and how the incumbent may face a significantly different requirement from the customer at the rebid let's look briefly at the facilities management outsourcing market. Over the past 15 years this market has changed dramatically in terms of what customers wish to procure from suppliers. Fifteen or so years ago the market was dominated by customer requirements for individual services, such as cleaning, catering, security, maintenance, etc. Customers tended more often to purchase on a local or regional geographical basis, with large customers often procuring separately for individual sites. Over the intervening period some of the major changes in procurement patterns include:

- Customers have increasingly 'bundled' different services into a single requirement, with a significant proportion of the market now being for 'total FM' – the provision of all services under a single contract.

- Larger customers with multiple sites are increasingly procuring for regional, national or even international contracts to cover all sites with a single contract and supplier.

- Performance measures have moved from input-based measures to output- or even outcome-based measures – some customers link facilities management contracts to their end-user experience and satisfaction – for instance some retailers, banks, hotels, etc. – as the services provided by contractors can increasingly involve the 'front of house' elements of the customer's service, such as security and reception, as well as how the ambience of the customer's premises is linked to its brand. Others are starting to see the positive impact that a good building environment and efficient services can have on the productivity and motivation of their own staff and are requiring contractors to focus on these and show how they will improve these areas.

- Real estate or estate management has started over the past five or more years to be bundled with Facilities Management, with single suppliers looking after the procurement, leasing and disposal of buildings for customers as well as the management of facilities. Some customers have even gone so far as to sell parts of or even their entire estate to a supplier and then lease it back fully serviced.

- Workspace planning and design has also become part of the customer's requirements for some FM contracts, with not only the physical layout of workspaces being a capability required of contractors, but process management changing radically for a range of services – whilst physical post is declining as email and electronic communication grows, this moved from locally managed to central post-delivery, sorting and distribution formats for some customers.

- Some Government customers have linked Facilities Management with Construction through the Private Finance Initiative (PFI), with single contracts for the financing of construction, facilities management and lifecycle maintenance for 25 or 30 years for a new building. The ability to design and build a building to make the ongoing FM more effective and efficient has often been a key winning factor in PFI contracts.

- The level of technology involved in Facilities Management contracts has changed dramatically, with, for instance, building management systems monitoring and controlling temperatures, lighting and security of buildings as well as a whole range of other elements. And within almost all service areas technology has impacted on services and how they can more effectively and efficiently be delivered.

- Areas of work that would in the past have been the remit of the IT team or contractor are beginning to be included in Facilities Management contracts as the level of technology in the work environment increases. For instance, networked photocopying and printing, video conferencing, IT Help desks are now all parts of many FM contracts.

- Requirements to be environmentally sustainable and reduce waste and consumption are increasingly important parts of FM contracts – not only in delivering the core services themselves in an environmentally friendly way, but taking on the energy management and reduction in energy and water use (both reducing the impact on the environment and helping customer's Corporate Social Responsibility agendas, but also saving them considerable costs) as well as reducing waste and improving recycling for the customer themselves.

All of these and other changes to customer requirements have happened over the past decade and a half. For a five-year contract that is the period of only three rebids. Whilst not all changes are requirements of all contracts, to continue to be competitive and meet the needs of customer's changing requirements suppliers have to change their own capabilities to match. Of course this is just one of many areas of outsourcing that are changing. Descriptions of other areas would show similar or even greater levels of change. For instance, Information Technology (central servers, through networks of PCs to the 'cloud' – and much else), Business Processes (centralized services and increased technology through to offshoring). Whichever industry you serve, the world is changing though the period of the contract and your customer's requirements at the end of the contract may be very different to those at the start.

DIRECTORS NOTE 3

This chapter raises a number of issues that need to be addressed by the Director across the contract portfolio:

> Gaining an understanding the changing needs of customers

> Keeping the business up to date with the changing best practice in the supply industry

> Deciding on the best commercial solutions regarding the level of investment in introducing changes to delivery within contracts or across the contract portfolio to address the above two drivers

Changing Needs of Customers

No two customers are exactly the same. But if your contract portfolio is based on one sector or industry, there are likely to be trends or changes that will impact to a varying degree across all or most of the customers within that sector. This might be a change in legislation, changes in market conditions for the customer, the introduction of new government policy or initiatives, or simply the dissemination of ideas or trends through industry forums. Evidence of these changes may not be obvious in any one contract, or particular customers may react to them differently and so each contract on its own may not gain a sense of the wider picture.

Also, within each industry or sector there will be some customers (perhaps not your own!) who are more proactive: Taking a lead in introducing or pushing for new, innovative ways of working, or focusing on particular areas of interest or strategic direction. These can sometimes be difficult and demanding customers to deal with, but they can give a great advantage to those working with them in that they force the introduction of new ways of working that less dynamic or innovative customers will only slowly or later come to address. The supplier who has the experience of working with the market leading customers can then bring these new and perhaps better ways of working to those customers who are following, thus gaining an advantage over the suppliers who have not been exposed to or pushed into these innovations.

As a director with a portfolio of contracts, the task in ensuring that your company is not left behind, and can gain a lead on competitors in reacting to changes in customer needs, can be addressed both from a top-down and bottom-up approach.

Top-down information will most likely come from strategic planning processes or the marketing or market analysis team if you have one. Gaining bottom-up information is likely to come from your own meetings and conversations with customers, but also from putting in place across the contract portfolio a planned approach to the analysis of their individual customer's changing needs and creating a process to collate and analyse the different needs being relayed from individual customers, bearing in mind the potential overall trends.

Best Practice in the Supply Industry

Most companies keep at least an eye on their direct competitors, however looking across the whole industry for best practice and new techniques can require a more determined and focused effort. In some industries it is the supply side that leads innovation, but in others there is a close correlation between the developments of customer needs and the offerings of the supply side. However, as mentioned above, there will be leading customers who will be demanding new and better services or products. Ensuring that your company is kept up to date on these developments will help understand where the industry might be leading. It is also helpful to keep a wider view on related industries. In the example given above on the facilities management industry, the developments have led to what were separate groups of often specialist suppliers that previously only looked to their direct equivalents as competitors, such as catering or cleaning organizations, joining up either through organic development of new products within companies, through subcontracting or through acquisition to create multi-service companies capable of delivering bundled services. More recently, the real estate industry and the facilities management industry have started in places to merge, with leaders from each industry acquiring capabilities or companies from the other. The largest facilities management companies are now competing for real estate opportunities, with the larger real estate market leaders taking on facilities management work within the portfolio of properties they manage through building or buying their own FM capabilities. Ensuring that your company has the capabilities required for the next set of rebids will demand forward thinking and taking a view of the wider industry, as well as putting in place plans and actions to enable your company to continue to compete as the industry changes. This may involve the company as a whole investing in new technology or new skills sets. It may involve major strategic decisions about the direction of the business and/or the need and ability of the business to invest in building, partnering or acquiring these capabilities to remain relevant in the industry.

Investment in Existing Contracts

Balancing the requirement to deliver a continuing and usually growing profit stream from existing contracts with the need to invest in developing those contracts to deliver to the customer continuous improvement, added vale and looking to introduce new ways to keep the contract relevant for the changes that may come in the rebid is a difficult task. Shareholders and Chief Executives expect to see growing levels of profit and both they and Finance Chiefs will usually question decisions to sacrifice profit in the short term on a contract in order to increase the longevity of the relationship with the customer. The cost in the short term is measurable and definite, correlating this with definite longer term gains is usually open to challenge.

Planning this investment ahead, over future financial periods, can help in socializing across your senior team the reasoning for this investment, and the costs can potentially be offset in future planning periods by new wins which bring in future profit streams. It may be that investment in different ideas should be spread across the contract portfolio, with ideas used on only one or two contracts until the positive customer response can be shown and presented, and then spreading these proven best practices across the contract portfolio. It may be that investment is required centrally to develop ideas, thus placing costs within the 'overhead' or divisional costs of the business rather than focusing them within contracts and reducing their gross margin contribution. Again this will require careful planning and clarity of purpose. Some larger businesses have created centres of excellence or best practice where experts in a particular field pull together the latest and most advanced ways to deliver services or reduce costs of services or products which can be used to win new business – but can potentially also be used to deliver improved services on existing contracts.

It may also be possible, by reviewing carefully rebid wins and losses to be able to build feedback in from customers to add to the strength of your argument of the benefits of investing now to gain future benefit.

For longer term contracts some companies have introduced 'mid-term reviews'. These involve a full review of the contract half way through its term, bringing in an external team to work through many of the techniques covered in later chapters of this book. These techniques are usually used at the rebid to check whether the contract still meets the needs of the customer as they have evolved over the intervening period since it was won and reviews the cost and structure of the contract to see if savings can be made. The team then reports back to the senior contract team and the operations management team within the business or division where the contract sits with their recommendations on what could be done to revitalize the contract. Whilst this should not necessarily replace an ongoing process of change and development, it can focus the minds of people within the business and create a 'burning platform' of issues that have been found not as they could be in order to galvanize a programme of changes and development on the contract but to bring it back into line with best practice. For a more detailed explanation on running a mid-term review, see the outline at the end of this chapter.

Whichever way the investment is made in delivering improving services through the life of existing contracts the benefit across the business portfolio of contracts will be felt over time as rebid retention rates increase and new contract wins grow the business rather than replace lost contracts.

Chapter 5 Checklist:

- Regularly review the market for changes and innovations.

- Keep in touch with changes and ambitions within the customer's organization.

- Review the potential for making changes to the contract within the contract period.

- Look to make carefully costed changes that fit with the customer's changing needs and demonstrate your ongoing innovation.

The Mid-term Review

The mid-term review has been mentioned in this chapter as a means of helping to keep a contract relevant. Below is a description of how to run a mid-term review.

PURPOSE

To review a longer term contract half way through its life in order to ensure that it is on track, and that it is still relevant to customer requirements and delivering to customer expectations

OUTCOME

A written review of the contract situation presented to senior managers with recommendations for changes that will put the contract on track for a successful second half of the contract period and success at rebid

WHO SHOULD RUN THE REVIEW?

This will depend on the size and importance of the contract. For a small contract the minimum will be two people, however for a larger contract up to four people may be required, depending on the time that managers wish the review to take. The review should be undertaken by people external to the contract. These can be sourced from a number of places within the company, or an external research agency or audit consultancy can be used. For larger businesses there may be an internal audit function that can be utilized. Usually there will be a lead reviewer supported by a financial expert who will work through the contract costs, Profit and Loss, balance sheet if appropriate and other aspects such as debtors, payroll, etc. Equally, an HR or Business Process Re-engineering expert may be used in addition, together with HR or organizational design experts if the contract size and complexity warrants. These may be supported by technical experts if the contract entails specialist elements or potentially large areas of information technology.

HOW LONG WILL THE REVIEW TAKE?

Again this will depend on the size and complexity of the contract and the availability of staff and the customer. For a smaller contract the review may take only a week. For a significantly larger contract the review may take over a month.

WHAT WILL BE COVERED AND IN WHAT ORDER?

1. The first area will be a review of the original contract and specification set out by the customer, together with any official change notices that have been put in place, to review what the base line is for the contract. This will be reviewed against the reality of what is required and what is being delivered at the mid-term point.

2. A review of the contract organization, structure, costs and staffing levels.

3. A review of profitability on the contract, and which elements of the contract this is being delivered from.

4. A review of the processes and systems in place on the contract and their performance, appropriateness and contribution to the overall efficiency and effectiveness of the contract.

5. A review of the measures in place and the performance against these.

6. Interviews with key staff and managers within the contract. Questions will vary depending on the type of contract but will cover areas such as:

    – The perceived level and type of relationship with the customer.
    – The performance of the contract in meeting its aims.
    – What is going well on the contract.
    – What has exceeded expectations.
    – What is not going so well on the contract.
    – Perceived reasons for the above.

7. Interviews with key customer staff and managers. These should include senior managers who are not directly involved in day to day contact with the contract. Questions here should focus on two areas:

    a) The customer's present situation, drivers, plans for the future and wider issues and ambitions
    b) The customer's view of the contract, including:

        i.   The perceived level of performance vs original expectations.
        ii. The relevance of the work being delivered now to the present needs of the customer, and how future changes in the customer's needs may or may not be delivered through the contract as it presently stands.
        iii. Any areas that the customer feel are particularly good about the contract and its delivery.
        iv. Any thoughts on improvements that could be made to the contract and its performance.
        v.   Perceived reasons for the above.

8.   If appropriate it may be useful, if they not already in place and being conducted regularly, to conduct surveys of staff and of end-users opinions and satisfaction with the contract and its management – though this may take some time and add to the cost of the review.

COLLATING INFORMATION AND WRITING THE REVIEW

Once all of the various sources of information have been looked at and the information collected and collated there will next be a period of analysis. There may be a requirement to recheck some of the information if it is either seen to be incomplete or contradictory.

From this work initial views and conclusions can start to be drawn and tested. Again these may require further information in specific areas, and thoughts may need to be tested by going back to people or other sources – though at this stage it should be made clear that these are initial ideas.

Finally a set of conclusions and recommendations can be drawn up. These will generally be under the following headings:

- An introduction to the contract and customer.

- The customer's position, changes in requirement since the start of the contract, aspirations plans and future requirements.

- The performance of the contract to date, against original requirements and against present customer requirements.

- The cost and profitability of the contract, and the effectiveness of its organization, processes, people and systems.

- Strong areas of the contract – particularly those that may have lessons or implications for what could be done on other contracts.

- Areas of weakness, in terms of performance and particularly against the customer's requirements and the perception of the customer.

- Recommendations for improvements to the contract now and changes over the remaining period of the contract to put it in the best position for the rebid.

The length and level of detail that the report goes into will vary with the size and complexity of the contract. The report may go into a range of specific areas of the contract and, especially if the contract delivers a range of different products or services, or is delivered in multiple geographies or from multiple bases, each may be dealt with under sub headings. If the company has a number of similar contracts and mid-term reviews become a standard part of the company's processes, then standard templates may be created with standardized marking schemes, or traffic light (red, amber and green) summaries of different aspects that can help comparisons between contracts. However, if this is the case it should be noted that over standardization can itself be a danger in that the review can become a box ticking exercise that only looks at set areas of the contract rather than digging into the unique areas of each contract to identify the specifics of its situation.

PRESENTING THE REVIEW

The final report will have a number of stakeholders interested in its contents and conclusions:

- Senior management and directors above the contract level will most likely be the primary stakeholders who have commissioned the review. The full report will be presented to them and it will largely be their decisions that impact on any changes that are to be implemented as a result.

- The contract team will also be very interested in the report and its conclusions and recommendations – it is after all their performance that is being commented on. How the company disseminated the report or versions of it will vary from company to company (and to a degree the level of performance that the report reveals). However the senior management team within the contract should certainly be given access to the report and the decisions of senior management will usually be made with the contract teams involvement.

- The customer is also very likely to be interested in the result of the review. They will almost certainly have needed to be informed of the review, certainly in order to gain access to those on the customer side who have been interviewed as part of the process. This can usually be introduced as a positive company process that is aimed at ensuring the contract is on track as part of the incumbents determination to ensure that they are delivering the best possible performance and service to the customer. It is likely that a presentation may be the best form of communication with the customer regarding the report, giving a summary of the findings and of the proposed plans for any changes that may have been decided or are preferred. The customer will in most cases wish to sign off on these and it is likely that any proposed changes will need to be 'sold' to the customer, either as resolutions to issues that the customer has fed into the process or as ideas for further improvement of delivery.

- Finally it may be that a wider cross section of staff on the contract should also be given a summary of the report, and any proposed improvements. They will have their own views and changes are likely to involve them in some way. Giving them an understanding of the reasons for any changes will be useful – and certainly any positive elements of the report should also be disseminated across the contract team.

6

Customer Relationships

At rebid the incumbent should have a significant advantage in that they have had the opportunity to develop a range of customer relationships over the contract period. These relationships should be used to gain as much information as possible on the customer's intentions, and of course having positive relationships within the evaluation team should help in ensuring the contract is retained.

However, there are a number of prerequisites that need to be fulfilled in order to make the most of these relationships:

- The relationships have to be with the relevant people in the customer organization.

- They have to be positive relationships (just because you know them, doesn't mean they are positively disposed towards you).

- The relationships need to be maintained through the contract period.

- The relationships need to be used carefully.

Building and Managing Relationships

It is going to be a natural part of running the contract that relationships with different people will be built up over the contract period. These will be at a number of levels within the customer organization, and will be held by a number of people within the incumbent – from the manager or director in charge of the contract, through to front-line staff and at most points in between. They will have been built up through the day to day running of the contract and the interactions that go with this delivery. All have potential to be useful to some degree during the rebid period.

However, because the rebid is unlikely to be conducted purely by the normal operational staff and managers that you dealt with during the contract they are not going to be the full picture. As with the original bid it is likely that other departments from within the customer's organization will be involved in their preparation and running of the rebid. For instance:

- If the customer has a procurement team, these will be involved.

- If the customer is changing the scope of the contract, it is likely that this will have been discussed at senior level, and these senior managers may have ongoing input into the rebid.

- The finance team may also be involved.

- If the customer is from the public sector there may be some overview from a central purchasing or audit body that governs procurement activity.

- There may be external consultants used by the customer to help with or even run large parts of the procurement exercise.

These are often groups that are not involved in the day to day running of the contract, and so the incumbent operational team may not have built up a relationship with them. Depending on the management arrangements that you have as a business there may be managers that are tasked with building these wider relationships within the customer organization, if not then you need to decide who will build and maintain these relationships. This is important because no matter how good a relationship you may have on the ground with the local customer manager of the contract they may have limited influence when it comes to rebid. Particularly if the customer is large they may at a senior level wish to significantly change the contract parameters for corporate or strategic reasons (which the local customer contact may not even be aware of). This could mean that the incumbent is caught out by a major change in the type or scope of contract at rebid, or misread the key evaluation criteria that the customer will use in the rebid. Potentially the advice they receive from their local management contacts in the customer may itself be misinformed or partial, and attempting to please the local manger may backfire if their aims are different to the senior decision makers and/or they themselves have little influence on the final decision.

It is likely that the type of customer managers and departments involved in the rebid will also have been involved in the original procurement exercise that was won to become an incumbent. This is a good starting point and it is wise to maintain these relationships wherever possible. As you go through the initial contract bidding process, note who is involved and what their roles are. When the contract is won, allocate who within your business will be tasked with maintaining these relationships and at what level (i.e. how frequently they should be met and communicated with). If your business has other contracts with the wider customer organization (or wants to have in the future), some of the central department contacts may be relevant for these, and so any relationship should be looked at in this light as well.

EXAMPLE 1

A National Health Service (NHS) Trust in the UK used a consultant to act as a facilitator helping to create their rebid evaluation process. The incumbent used their contacts with the customer to find out who the consultant would be and on studying the consultant's website found that they had written a book on procurement processes. The incumbent bought the book and studied it finding out in the process that the consultant set out a very particular and detailed procedure for managing procurements. The rebid questions and process used by the customer followed the book almost exactly and, using this knowledge, the incumbent was able to both predict the questions being asked in presentations made at the final stages of the rebid, and reflect the consultant's language from the book in their rebid response. The rebid was won, with the customer commenting positively on how the incumbent had picked up the thinking of the team in answering the questions set.

RELATIONSHIP MAPPING

To be sure that you are building the right network of relationships to be of most impact at rebid it is useful to think through and plan who the right people in the customer organization are and what their roles might be at rebid. There are a number of methods for allocating roles to particular contacts in customers and for mapping the relationships that they have to the bid decision. These are most commonly used in the initial sales or bidding process for new business and are covered in many books on sales and on a range of sales training courses. These methods are as relevant for the period of the contract and for moving into the rebid period. The difference is the maintenance of the contacts over the contract period, the potential difference in their impact on the contract as it is running and their potentially different impact on the rebid itself. We will cover an outline of how these methods can be used below, but you should adapt the terminology or specifics to fit any existing process that you use in your business.

Typically in a sales process, customer contacts will be broken down into their potential roles in the decision making regarding the contract – sometimes as a group they will be called the 'decision making unit'. You will find variations of the role definition of those involved in different books, but essentially the roles are similar to those below:

- Decision makers – the people (or person) who makes the ultimate decision about which company is chosen for the contract, or whether the purchase/procurement is made.

- Influencers – those who have some influence on the decision of who is chosen, the method of procurement or the form of the contract.

- Coach – a contact, usually within the customer organization, who will actively support your efforts to win the contract.

Exactly who these people are and what their day to day jobs and titles are will vary from customer to customer and even within customers potentially from contract to contract.

To create a relationship map, start by listing who the key contacts are that you are aware of, and for each one of them add the following information:

- Job title.

- Role in the Decision Making Unit (decision maker, influencer).

- Required level of relationship.

- Actual relationship at present (unknown, poor, ok, good, etc.).

- What is important to them about the contract (price, quality, happy end-user, etc.).

- How well they think we are achieving this at present.

- Who the best person is in our organization to lead our relationship with them.

- How we are going to keep/build our relationship with them.

- How we are going to ensure they have a positive attitude towards us during the contract and at the rebid.

This initial list should be created early in the contract and reviewed regularly to check how it is progressing. Whilst some of the relationships will build naturally through the day to day interactions that you have as a team in running the contract, others may require an additional and planned effort that may not be of obvious day to day use in the general running of the contract. But bear in mind that these contacts will be difficult to create from scratch towards the end of the contract as the rebid approaches so they are worth the effort.

Of course, over a longer term contract some of these contacts will most likely change; people get promoted, change jobs or leave and new contacts will need to be built. Keeping a regular review of your list (and adding to it as you gain new information) will help to ensure that you do not lose track of who you need to be talking to, how you are thought of by these people and what you need to do to keep abreast of those who will impact on keeping the contract. You might want to add this as a part of monthly team meetings, or as a part of any regular reviews that you do of the contract or contract performance.

To better understand and manage the relationships you are building during the contract it is useful to look at how the people you are talking with relate to each other. Just as in your own business, people in the customer organization don't exist in a vacuum – they work with each other and have different levels and quality or relationships with each other. Understanding these relationships can help you understand the different influences that your contacts might have on the rebid.

A simple way of understanding formal relationships within the customer organization is to look at the customer organization chart. This will give you

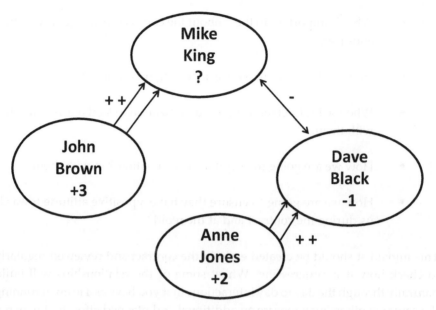

Figure 6.1   Simplified relationship map showing stakeholders' view of
the contract and their relationships

some sense of roles, hierarchy and decision making routes. But, just as in your own business, this is far from the full picture. You need to understand the real relationships between the people on your list and the politics in the customer organization in order to get the full picture of who has influence on who and to what extent. You can keep track of this through notes on your listing of contacts, or by using a diagram such as Figure 6.1 (you can create it as a team using a white board or post it notes).

In Figure 6.1, John Brown has a positive attitude towards you as a supplier (+3) and a strong and positive relationship with Mike King (2 '+'). Anne Jones is also positive towards you (+2) and has a strong positive relationship with Dave Black. Dave Black has a negative view towards you (-1) and a weak negative relationship with Mike King (one '-'). You don't presently know Mike King's view of you.

Knowing the above, could you get introduced to Mike King (who for our purpose here might be a senior director not directly involved in your contract but with an influence on the rebid) by John Brown? Or work with Anne Jones to improve Dave Black's view of you? Or perhaps if you cannot gain a relationship with Mike King, the positive influence of John Brown will inform Mike King's view more than Dave Black's influence?

You should also look beyond the direct customer organization when building relationships. There may be others who will impact on the rebid, such as consultants bought in to help with the rebid process. Consultants can have a significant impact on the rebid process especially with customers who may not have great experience of managing rebids. In some cases they will work as facilitators, helping the customer to create a clear rebid process, thinking through the evaluation process, scoring, etc. In some cases rebids can be almost entirely outsourced to a consultancy organization, with the customer only getting involved at the final stages with scoring of final documents, or even making the final decision from recommendations made by the consultant. Using your customer relationships to find out if a consultant will be used and who they will be can give you the opportunity to get to know the consultant, or at least study their preferred processes and approach.

EXAMPLE 2

A contractor delivering facilities management services to a major retailer changed their contract manager twice during the three-year contract period. The customer had also changed their own managers over the contract period. As a result relationships that had been built up on a positive basis in the early period of the contract were lost and never recovered. The new customer managers had a different view of how the contract should be run and formed a poor view of the supplier who was delivering as had originally been agreed, but had not innovated during the contract period. When the rebid came around the supplier had few relationships to draw on and limited positive views within the customer of their performance during the contract. The contract was lost at rebid.

Who Should Manage Relationship Management?

In order to ensure that relationship management is conducted in a coherent and planned way it is useful for the incumbent to have a plan for how they wish to build and maintain relationships with the customer and to place overall responsibility for the delivery of this plan in the remit of a particular individual. This, of course, does not mean that the individual chosen is the person who has to build all of the relationships. Their role is to ensure that there is a plan, that relevant people in the business know their own roles in this plan, that each relationship and information gained from it is captured and that the plan is driven forward and regularly reviewed.

Different businesses in different sectors and circumstances tend to use different people and roles to fulfill this function. If the contract involved is with a large customer, there are multiple contracts with the customer, or the contractor has a range of other services that the customer may procure that are not presently within existing contracts, then using an account manager may be appropriate. The account manager will not usually have operational responsibility for the existing contracts, but will be focussed more on building relationships across the customer at levels that will both help with the existing contract rebids, but will also be aimed at the successful winning of new contracts or extension of the products or services provided within existing contracts. This is not to say that the account manager should not be able to influence the operational delivery of the existing contracts. If through the relationships built up the account manager finds that the customer is either not content with aspects of the existing delivery, or is looking for changes to how existing contracts are delivered, or perhaps discovers that the customer is anticipating procuring in a different way for the next contract period, then they should be able to work with the operational leads to ensure that the contract is changed or adapted to meet these needs.

In other circumstances, for instance, where the contract dominates the potential for business with the customer, the contract manager with operational responsibility for delivery of the contract may also be the lead for relationship management. This will, however, mean that the contract manager must have the skills, and make the time, to build and maintain relationships with those within the customer who may not be directly involved on a day to day basis with the contract, but who may be important in the rebid. Whoever is responsible for relationship management should be working to a plan for the customer relationship which will include aspects such as:

- Who do we want to have a relationship with?

- What information do we need from this contact?

- What do we want this contact to think and feel about the contract and contractor?

- What actions may we want this contact to take that will help us?

This should ideally be written down in a clear plan that covers the overall aims of the incumbent, the short and medium term actions to be taken regarding relationships, measures the progress of these actions, and records key meetings and what is said to and by the contacts in meetings with different people from the contractor. There should also be a history kept of these plans, meetings and information, perhaps on a Contact Management System so that the progress of the relationship can be kept in one place, perhaps with other information gleaned about the customer, reviewed and if the relationship manager moves to other roles or leaves the business there is a clear record of what has been done and said.

Chapter 6 Checklist:

- Note the customer departments and people involved in the original bid.

- Build a database of customer contacts.

- Allocate your own people to build relationships with these contacts.

- Regularly review the state of relationships and any changes in customer personnel.

- Think about who will be involved in the rebid outside of your normal contacts.

- Remember that consultants may be involved.

Preparing for and Running a Successful Rebid

7

Rebid Preparations

It should be obvious from reading this book so far that as the incumbent you should be putting thought and effort into preparing for the rebid from day one of the contract. However, at some point in the contract, as the rebid comes closer, these preparations should take on more urgency and significant time and resources should be directed at preparing for the process of winning the rebid.

When should this increase in urgency take place and how should you ensure that you have the right resources, information and plan in place to be ahead of the game when the rebid commences in earnest?

The Customer's Preparations

It is worth looking at the stages that the rebid will go through from the customer's perspective as they decide on the pace of the programme and of course run the process (sometimes with help from outside consultants).

A simple way of estimating the likely programme is to start with the final date of the contract as set out in the original contract and work backwards through each stage of the customer's rebid process. Table 7.1 sets out a hypothetical timetable for a rebid. It will of course change depending on the size of the contract and its overall length and the specific stages may vary depending on the market sector you are in or the type of service or product you are supplying. However, it is worth going through this exercise early in the contract.

There are some rules regarding the minimum time that Government customers can give for the formal process from publication of OJEU (in Europe) to contract finish depending on the size of the contract, but even within this

Table 7.1   Example of a customer rebid timetable

Activity or point in the process	Potential length of time	Cumulative count back from last day of the contract (weeks)
Last day of the existing contract	1 day	0
Phase in of the new contract/ contractor	6 weeks	-6
Final negotiations	3 weeks	-9
Chosen contractor confirmed	1 day	-
Stand still period	2 weeks	-11
Chosen contractor published	1 day	-
Customer evaluating final bids	2 weeks	-13
Final bids delivery date	1 day	-
Contractors preparing final bids	4 weeks	-17
Final stage documents published to shortlisted contractors	1 day	-
Customer evaluating initial bids (PPQ/RFP) and choosing shortlist	2 weeks	-19
Initial bids delivery date	1 day	-
Contractors preparing initial bids	4 weeks	-23
Initial bid documents published	1 day	-
Period for contractors to express interest	3 weeks	-25
Customer publicises rebid (in Europe for Government contracts on OJEU)	1 day	-
Customer deciding on evaluation process and preparing documentation for the rebid	5 weeks	-30
Customer agreeing on the breadth of the new contract and its form	7 weeks	-37
Customer deciding on the requirements of the new contract	6 weeks	-43

there is some opportunity for the customer to vary the specific processes undertaken and the length of time given for different parts of the process.

In this hypothetical example (see Table 7.1) the formal bid started 25 weeks prior to the contract finish date (about six months). For your rebid this time could be shorter or longer. You may wish to look at the previous bid for the contract for some guidance on the possible length and format the customer used, though of course this may change next time. However, the point that is sometimes missed by incumbent teams is the period of time prior to this during which the customer is making a large number of decisions about the future contract and the form of the rebid process, documentation and evaluation scoring – in the example this work started 18 weeks (about four months) before the formal bid process.

In fact the UK Office of Government Commerce (OGC) advice to Government Departments on contract re-competition has been that they should start preparing for rebid between 18 months and four years before the end of a contract (depending on size, duration and criticality of the contract). At this time the advice given has been to undertake a strategic assessment of the contract and what the Department wishes to procure for the next contract period.

Whether this is a government or private sector customer this time is hugely important for the rebid because it is when the customer is determining what they want the next contract to deliver, what form it should take, how they will run the procurement, what they are going to evaluate potential contractors against and what payment regime they want to have. It may be that the customer decides not to make many changes from the previous contract procurement and type of service or product they want. But as was discussed in Chapter 5 ('Keeping the Contract Relevant'), it may be that they are deciding on radical changes to all aspects.

The customer (or contacts within the customer with whom you have built a strong relationship) might talk to you about this process, but more often than not the process is undertaken internally without involving the incumbent. In fact public sector organizations are specifically advised against involving the incumbent in these discussions.

> *Ensure that the incumbent does not assist with the specification of the new contract. An external expert (sourced competitively and excluded from bidding for the main contract) may be required to do this work.*
>
> *(Office of Government Commerce (OGC) Guidance Paper*
> *on Contract Re-competition)*

This is the point where your relationship building with customer contacts, how well you have delivered the contract, adapted to changes in the customer's needs and innovated over the period of the contract will potentially give you an advantage. You are more likely to gain an insight into the customer's thinking and process if they respect you and want to do business with you in the future. Having an opportunity to understand the emerging customer strategy for the rebid and the next contract period will be vital in your own preparations.

Having an understanding of what the customer is looking for in the next contract period not only gives you a chance to prepare for how you will deal with the rebid process itself; it can give you a chance to demonstrate your ability to deliver any emerging needs that the customer may have and be looking for in the next contract period. You might achieve this by showing the customer where you are already delivering them in other contracts. A more effective approach will be to pilot or introduce any new ways of working or approaches that the customer is looking for in the future on the existing contract over the months prior to the rebid. If you are providing IT or a product it may also give you time to develop any changes, upgrades or new features that the customer is looking for (see the section in Chapter 9 on Green Field Review).

This will be particularly important if the customer is looking for significant changes or improvements to the scope or delivery of the contract. One of the potential disadvantages for the incumbent is that the customer may believe that they know the full extent of your capabilities based on what you are presently delivering and have delivered over the contract. They may have seen other contractors delivering on contracts more akin to the type of contract they are aiming to have in the next period (or of course these contractors may have been actively marketing to the customer for a period of time) and believe they are more suited to the new contract than your company. You will need to expand their understanding of what you are capable of delivering to overcome this possible prejudice.

It is therefore important if you, as the incumbent, wish to avoid missing out on the opportunity to influence, or at least be aware of, the customer's decision making process regarding the rebid, that you start your rebid preparations before this time and have in place a plan, even if in outline, and set responsibilities for named individuals within the business for putting the early stages of this plan into action.

Who Will Run the Rebid For You?

Companies vary in the person, team or department given responsibility for winning their rebids. Some will give the responsibility to the contract or account manager who has been running the contract or who has responsibility for managing the relationship with, and growth of, the customer account. Others see rebid responsibility as being part of business development and responsibility is passed onto a bidder who may normally be focussed on winning new business.

Each of these roles have certain advantages and potential disadvantages regarding being in charge of the rebid – of course the capabilities, experience and skills of the individual will also vary, but given this:

The contract manager has the advantage of having (hopefully) an intimate understanding of the contract and a direct relationship with at least the operational customer. However, unless they have created a strong team who can run the contract with little input during the rebid period, they may struggle to properly fulfil both tasks in what will be a frenetic period. They may also not be familiar with the details of how rebid process works and how to run a rebid having spent the past years running an operation rather than bidding. There is also a danger that the contract manager will not have the breadth of experience of other ways of delivering services or of new developments in the market to be able to bring new and radical thinking to the solution for the new contract. Or indeed they may have the view that as the contract is presently running successfully and they have a strong team that they have good relationships with will be disinclined to feel that significant and potentially painful changes or reductions in costs are needed to win. Particularly if there is likely to be a significant change in the customer requirement they may not have the objective view required to make significant changes to the contract – which may not include themselves as the best person to run the new contract.

A bid manager will have the advantage of being familiar with running bid processes and delivering bid documents and solutions. The potential issue here is the amount of time that the bid manager is given to get to know the detail of the contract and prepare the rebid. There should be a larger amount of information available at rebid than for a normal bid that can and should be used to show the incumbent's capability and performance over the contract period. If the bidder is not given sufficient time to collate and use this, then it will be lost to the rebid effort. At the same time, the relationships that the contract team have built up must also be effectively used. The bidder must be able to work effectively through the team, or gain their own relationships with the customer – especially those in the customer organization who may not be involved day to day in the contract but will have influence on the rebid.

In reality, for all but the smaller rebids, a team approach is required as a number of different skills will be needed together with knowledge of, and contact with, the customer. Whichever department, team or individual is ultimately responsible there are certain tasks and roles that need to be undertaken and fulfilled as part of the preparation and running of the rebid and a mix of bid and operational staff will be required to participate if it is to be successful.

Rather than give a set recommendation on who your particular business should be tasked to lead the rebid (as different organizations will have different structures) I suggest that the team, wherever they are drawn from should have the capabilities, experience and influence within the business to achieve the tasks, loosely be grouped into four headings, set out below:

Information: Gathering and using of information about the contract, competitors and the customer – especially customer future requirements – to guide and inform the rebid and to use within the rebid document.

Bid process: Managing the rebid process, setting out a timetable and actions for different individuals and delivering the rebid documentation, pricing, presentations etc., on time and to the required specification.

Solution management: Creation of a solution for how the contract will be organized, managed, and delivered in the next period. This will involve commercial and financial elements as well as design of the organization, systems and processes and a particular focus in most cases of how to reduce costs of delivery and the price to the customer.

Change management: Putting in changes to the existing contract delivery or performance that move towards the new solution if possible prior to the rebid. Planning the transition from the existing contract organization and processes etc., to the new solution.

All of these groupings of work, of course, must fully interact with each other and should not be worked on in isolation. For instance, there is little point in creating a new solution without having and using as much information as possible about the customer's future aims and intentions and it would be ineffective to attempt to write the rebid in isolation from either the information about the contract and customer requirements or a clear understanding of the new solution.

Equally none of the above tasks are one-off exercises – all will involve iterative work that will, over the rebid period, inform the other areas and tasks to bring out a clear focus on the best final outcome.

Whatever the size and composition of your team you should ensure that those who are to be involved are identified early and are given plenty of time, as a team, to fully get involved with the contract, understand the present composition and performance of the contract to date and understand as well as possible the customer and their needs.

They will also need to be organized under the rebid leader (who will work with them to devise the rebid strategy and work towards its delivery), and potentially back filled in their existing roles for the duration of their involvement in the rebid – potentially part time in the early days, but full time as the rebid progresses.

Chapter 7 Checklist:

- Gain an early understanding of the customer's rebid timetable and preparations.

- Put in place the right rebid team as early as possible.

8

The Rebid Strategy

The first task of the rebid team leader will be to set out a high level Rebid Strategy. This will bring together, as with any strategy:

- A review of the situation.

- The outcome that you want to achieve.

- Your outline plan for achieving this outcome.

- And a more detailed programme of work streams and resources that will deliver the plan.

Having a strategy in place means that you have discussed, agreed and communicated to all those involved, both on the rebid team and the operational team on the contract. This should mean that there is clear buy-in from all involved of the task ahead and their roles within it, and clarity of the time available to complete the tasks required. Of course as with all strategies, the rebid strategy will need to be regularly checked to ensure that it is on track and that any changes in the situation surrounding the customer, contract and rebid are incorporated into your strategy and plans to achieve it. Below is a brief explanation of each of the elements listed.

Review of the Situation

This will include, but will not be limited to the areas already discussed in earlier chapters:

- The performance on the contract to date.

- A review of the customer – who does what, what are the customer's requirements and aims, what pressures are on the customer etc.

- The relationship that has been built with the customer – and crucially an assessment of how much the customer is in favour of retaining your services in the next contract period.

- The likely changes the customer will be making to the contract in the rebid.

- The effectiveness of the existing contract structure in delivering effectively and efficiently the customer's needs, and at the same time making a return for the company.

- Who are the likely competitors – what are their strengths and weaknesses.

- What has progressed in your company in the intervening period.

- What has changed in the market during the period of the contract – is new technology available, have trends in contract type changed? (For examples of this see Chapters 2 and 5.)

- Is there an option to extend the contract rather than go through a rebid – and is this the preferred option for the business?

- How prepared are you for the rebid – is the right team available, is the right information about the contract to date, the likely rebid format and the opportunities going forward to innovate, cut costs, and/or improve the contract performance already clear and obvious? Or are you starting from scratch and need to build this information quickly?

The Outcome You Want To Achieve

This may seem obvious at first glance – you want to win the rebid of course. But it is worth checking that this is actually the case – perhaps your business is moving into different areas, or the margin that the contract offers is no longer attractive, or perhaps the customer is a particularly difficult one that the cost of dealing with it is greater than the margin available is worth. Unlikely as it is that you will not wish to rebid, it is sensible to check all these factors so that you are going ahead with clarity.

Beyond this, you should check the particular outcomes that you want to achieve for the contract ahead – can you get an extension as has been mentioned above? Also, is there the opportunity to expand the scope of the contract, or deliver it in a new way? If these are options then you will need to be communicating with and influencing the customer to attempt to get the rebid specified in a way that will help you achieve these things.

Your Outline Plan For Achieving Your Outcomes

This will cover a number of key areas:

- The team and resources you need to deliver the rebid win.

- The rebid budget. This is something often not specifically set out in some businesses.

How much will your rebid cost you – in terms of people costs; potentially accommodation costs; costs of advisors, such as legal and commercial support; the cost of preparing the bid documentation, etc. Setting and managing a rebid budget effectively means that the business has clarity on the full costs and therefore returns of the contract:

- The timetable for the rebid process and the key dates by which specific actions need completion.

- The level of change that you will be addressing in the rebid and how you plan to find the best solution to win.

- Whether you will need to find partners or significant new subcontractors for the new contract.

- The review process for the rebid.

- The commercial aspects of the rebid, and if there is a sense of the price levels that you may need to achieve.

- Customer relationship management during the rebid.

- Timings and responsibilities for actions and how the rebid will be managed as a project.

Once the outline plan is completed this should be shared with the core team to be sure that everyone is aware of the requirements that the plan implies – making sure of course that you keep security around the plan so that competitors do not gain information that will be valuable to them.

More Detailed Work Streams

These will break down the overall tasks and set detailed timetables for each and allocate specific people to achieve them. The plan should be created on a project basis, perhaps with Gannt charts etc., to ensure that all aspects of the plan are coordinated and the critical path is clear. Depending on the size and complexity of the rebid you may need to allocate as part of the team a project coordinator who will keep the plan up to date, ensure that all elements of the work streams are progressing to plan, and ensure that the overall project plan is kept up to date and continues to be communicated to the team and remains viable in terms of delivering the rebid on time. Part of the detailed plan will be regular reviews of progress to ensure that you are on track and as new information becomes available the strategy is reviewed to ensure that it is still be best way to deliver the successful rebid.

With your team in place, your rebid strategy decided and a clear project plan in place you are now in a position to manage and deliver your rebid.

Chapter 8 Checklist:

- Start the rebid process in good time.

- Review the rebid situation.

- Create a clear Rebid Strategy and associated project plan for the rebid.

9

Preparing the Rebid Solution

Because of the amount and level of information that you as the incumbent should have, both of the customer's intentions and of the performance of the contract to date, you should aim to have decided on your rebid strategy, created an initial solution for the new contract period, and at least outline written documents for the rebid well before the official customer bid documentation is published. You will then be able to test the solution with the customer (or at least with any coach that you have within the customer organization) as early as possible. Having the core of your solution and proposal already decided and tested will give you additional time to refine your proposal once the rebid documentation is made available by the customer. Crucially as well, you will also be in a position to start to make any appropriate changes to the delivery of the existing contract that will be able to show the customer that you are able to deliver the new contract format and focus if this is appropriate.

Of course you must still remain able and open to changing the solution and presentation of your rebid to reflect the detail of the formal rebid requirements set by the customer – there can be a danger that having created a solution you feel reflects the needs of the customer you present this, rather than answering the specific questions asked in the rebid documentation. This is likely to lose you significant marks in any formal evaluation process. If you do see a difference between what your intelligence gained from customer contacts tells you and what is in the formal rebid then you must carefully test your contacts: are they really the key people who are going to decide the rebid decision, or do they really have the full story of what the customer is looking for; are they really committed to helping you win the rebid; are you properly interpreting what they are telling you?

There can be cases where the customer has been so keen to keep the existing incumbent they have put out a rebid document that any non-incumbent responding to compliantly would not win, however, these are rare and also dangerous for the incumbent.

Ideally you will be in a position before the documentation is released to have a good idea of what is in it and why. If there is a difference between the documentation and the questions, weighting and expectations expressed in the customer's documentation and your information you must check why with your contacts. When completing the rebid documentation the best approach will be if possible to answer the questions set compliantly and then put in an additional alternative solution and proposal and fully explain why this is a superior solution for the customer.

The Green Field Review

One of the key roles of the rebid leader, and of the rebid team, will be to take a critical view of the existing contract delivery organization. As we have mentioned in earlier chapters, the contract is not like a business no matter how entrepreneurial your organization, and no matter how many changes may have been made during the contract period. To some degree the contract has 'frozen' the terms of how the customer has had their service or product delivered for the period of the contract. Particularly over a longer contract period things will have changed in the marketplace – perhaps new technology, new methods of working or new pricing structures have emerged that are not in place on the existing contract. The customer, their circumstances and their needs will also most likely have changed, and these may not all have been able to be reflected within the existing contract. The new contract solution will need to take these into account if you are to be competitive.

At the same time within the contract organization things may have grown or developed in a particular way that has reflected the particular contract circumstances. Hopefully there are many positives – expertise will have grown in the tasks required, familiarity with the ways of working and continued efficiency drives will have cut the cost of many elements of delivery. But on the other hand, ways of working that are not fully efficient may also have grown. Costs in certain areas may have expanded: numbers of people involved may have grown, and levels of salaries may also have increased above market rates. Structures, processes and approaches may have emerged as 'the way we do things around here' or 'this is what the customer wants' that may need to change for the new contract, but which the existing team would either not see as needing to change or would resist changing if left to their own solution development. This inertia must be broken down if the new contract solution is to be the most competitive possible.

The Green Field Review takes the needs of the customer and ignores how your existing contract is organized. It starts from scratch and builds up a solution, organization, use of technology, set of partners or subcontracting relationships, set of processes, and commercial solution that best fits the needs of the customer for the next contract period – a completely Green Field solution.

The Green Field Review will normally require a different set of people to those presently working on the contract to avoid the assumptions that they have built up whilst working on the contract and the potential for them to ignore radically new ways of delivering the customer needs that may be entirely at odds with how the contract is presently organized. If your company has a team dedicated to creating new solutions then this is the group to use, failing that a team dedicated to new business development is more likely to be experienced at looking for the latest and most competitive solutions.

Of course, the Green Field solution, once it has been created, should not become the automatic default for your solution to the new contract period. Its other purpose is to test the existing way that you are running the contract for competitiveness. Once the Green Field solution has been created the rebid team should run a workshop with the existing contract team to test the relative benefits of what is presently being done and what the Green Field solution proposes. This can be an uncomfortable meeting and must be managed carefully. The existing team may be defensive about their existing way of doing things and their grasp of the detail of the existing contract may lead the solution to be watered down. They may also be understandably looking at the past and the present, rather than thinking about how things could radically change in the future and will also see many issues with getting from where the contract is to where the Green Field solution proposes rather than seeing a genuine review of the options based on the customer's future needs delivering the best possible combination of new thinking and existing knowledge. The rebid team must be able to separate out any such reticence from genuine insights that the existing contract team have in the practicalities of the contract, and take an objective view of whether any objections to the Green Field solution have a strong basis and so need to be properly taken into account.

The timing of the Green Field Review will depend on the amount of information that you have been able to glean from the customer about their future intentions before the official start of the competition. Ideally you should have a view before the customer goes officially to the market, and in this case the Green Field Review should be completed as early as possible. This will enable new ways of working that are identified to be tested on the existing contract if appropriate in order to get feedback from the customer and put you ahead of the competition.

Depending on the relationship you have with the customer, which hopefully if the contract has been run well is a good one, you may also decide to take the proposed Green Field solution to key contacts within the customer team. If you do decide to do this you should be clear on what you want to achieve. The outcome could be that the customer is impressed by the innovative approach you are taking and, at best in sectors where rebids are not legally required, they may ask you to implement the new structure and extend the contract period accordingly rather than having to go through a rebid. Alternatively the customer may take a number of your ideas and put them into the specification for the rebid – you need to be clear whether you see this as a potential benefit in giving you a specification based on a solution that you want to deliver and you understand well, or whether it is diluting your benefit over potential competitors by giving them a number of your best ideas for the contract.

Once you are clear on the best solution you are likely to take into the rebid you should also, as early as possible, work through a clear plan for how you will transform your existing contract into the new structure you are proposing. This will be vitally important in the rebid as this change brings risk to the customer during the period of transformation in terms of performance potentially dropping. Your plan should be carefully thought through – if possible tested with the customer. If you are confident that the customer is going to be looking for the changes you have proposed then you have the opportunity to start some of these prior to the rebid to get ahead of potential competitors.

There are three dangers to be aware of at this stage however:

1. You need to be confident that this change is genuinely what the customer will be looking for in the rebid – be sure you have spoken to those in the customer organization who are actually deciding on the new structure, rather than those who may be close to you

operationally but do not have decisive influence on the format of the new contract.

2.   During the period of change in moving aspects of your delivery to the new solution beware of any possible dip in performance. You do not want to put in changes that risk your performance on the contract falling just as the rebid is about to start – even if the customer is supportive of the changes you are making they may lose some confidence in your performance – at exactly the wrong time to guarantee rebid success.

3.   You need to be clear on the level of investment you are going to put into these changes prior to the rebid. How is this investment going to be accounted for? Will senior management within your company see this as a prudent investment and accept its value? Can it be taken out of contract profits and again, is this reduction acceptable within the business plan set for the contract and the wider business?

Once the specification for the new contract period is released the Green Field solution can be tested against these detailed needs and reviewed for practicality and competitive advantage it will bring. It can then be adapted to fit exactly what has been asked for in the rebid documentation. This then becomes the solution you are going to bring to the rebid.

Prepare a Set of 'Win Themes' For Your Rebid

Win Themes will be familiar to those experienced in bidding for new contracts. They are the key reasons that you will be putting into your rebid communication, bid documentation and presentations to the customer about why your company and solution are the best fit for their needs and deliver the maximum benefits for the customer.

Win Themes are just as important a part of a rebid as they are for a new bid, but there are a few common mistakes that can be made by rebid teams that you should avoid in deciding on and using your Win Themes for the rebid.

To be effective and persuasive there are a number of features that a good Win Theme should have:

- It must be relevant to a real and important customer need or requirement.

- It must deliver a demonstrable benefit to the customer to meet the need it is addressing.

- It must do so better than a competitor could, or is proposing to, deliver.

- Ideally it should be a Win Theme that is unique to you that a competitor could not deliver at all.

- You must show that it is deliverable and how you will deliver it in your solution over the coming period.

Ideally you will have a set of 4–6 key Win Themes that will flow through your solution and documentation. These will address the main needs of the customer and will be those that deliver the greatest and most unique benefit to the customer that your solution and company can deliver. These may be supplemented by a series of sub-Win Themes that address specific areas of your solution.

Win Themes don't usually appear by accident. You should conduct a clear review of the customer's needs (in line with your Green Field Solution review of needs) and work through how you can best deliver these needs. You should also spend time when generating your solution in working out what your Win Themes will be. This will be an iterative process. By identifying the needs of the customer you should look to create a solution that meets these needs – thus using potential Win Themes to influence what you will put in your solution. At the same time as you are creating your solution you will most likely identify areas that are important benefits and so should also be identified as potential Win Themes.

Be sure however not to let the list of Win Themes drift and multiply without keeping a clear grip on a list of those that are genuinely key to your solution and rebid.

SOME COMMON WIN THEME MISTAKES IN REBIDS

- Win Themes focus too much on the experience of the incumbent in the previous period. This is by far the most common mistake made by rebidders. Whilst the experience built up of the customer and of delivering the contract is a core strength of the incumbent, and of course should be used as part of the Win Themes, it is not itself sufficient to win the rebid. Look back for instance at the table in Chapter 4 of poorly written examples of statements used in rebids. Rather than a simple set of statements asserting that the experience built up in the contract will help the customer, Win Themes should use this experience to give evidence of how the company has used this experience to deliver quantifiable benefits to the customer to date – and crucially how this will enable the delivery of specific benefits or Win Themes in the coming contract.

- Win Themes are based on company capabilities – not on specific benefits that the solution is delivering to the customer. Too often when reviewing Win Themes they are found to be based on 'our company's experience in delivering this type of contract' or 'our company's unique culture'. Whilst again these may be behind benefits that are being delivered to the customer, they must lead to specific parts of the solution that are evidenced as delivering a specific and real benefit to the customer.

- Win Themes are generated from the solution at a late stage to be used in writing the rebid documentation – rather than being used to generate elements or aspects of the solution. As we have said above, generating Win Themes is an iterative process and some will emerge from your solution. But it is much more powerful to decide what the main Win Themes must be to win and then generate a solution that delivers them.

One technique to generate Win Themes is to set out the key customer needs and benefits that they wish to gain and then review your solution to understand where and how these needs are being met:

Customer needs	Aspects of our solution that deliver to these needs	Examples and evidence from the contract of how these are already delivered (if appropriate)

Be sure to list the needs first, then put in the aspects of your solution that meet them. Any gaps should push you to look carefully at how they can be filled with changes or additions to your solution.

An additional technique is to breakdown your list of Win Themes into the following boxes:

Benefits based on our company capabilities		
Benefits being delivered in our		
	Other competitors can deliver	**Unique to our business/solution**

When conducting this exercise ensure that you take a critical and objective view of your rebid Win Themes. If you have some Win Themes in the left hand side boxes this is not necessarily a bad thing – there may be essential requirements that the customer has that all competitors can deliver and that you must also be able to demonstrate. However, often rebid teams will find that, even at a relatively late stage in their rebid, the majority of their Win Themes are placed in the upper left box – benefits based on company capabilities that are not unique to the business. If this is the case then a review of the solution is required (not simply a restating of the Win Themes to make them sound unique). How can your solution be added to or changed to generate unique Win Themes, and how can you genuinely use your company capabilities in your solution to deliver real, quantifiable and evidenced benefits to the customer?

Your first review of Win Themes should be done well before the rebid documentation is published by the customer, as an early part of your rebid preparations. As the incumbent your relationships with and knowledge of your customer should be used to identify what their corporate and specific needs and drivers are, which should put you at an advantage over your competitors.

As the rebid process progresses and the customer specifications and ITT/ RFP are published you should also review these in detail. What are the specific requirements that are set out in these documents and how do your Win Themes help you answer the questions the customer has set? As will be covered in the next chapter you must combine your knowledge of the customer and the needs you understand they have through your work on the contract with what they have set out (and will be a part of their official evaluation and scoring of your rebid response) in their rebid documentation.

It is the effective combination of both of these elements that will help win the rebid. Not just answering the questions set (it can be a difficult task for a customer to fully and clearly elucidate all of their core needs in a specification document), but equally not ignoring the questions set and focusing only on core needs – as this may lose you marks in a more structured evaluation process.

You may also find it useful at an early stage to rerun your Win Theme exercise, but from the perspective of your competitors. Whilst you may not have a full understanding of all those who will bid for the contract it is likely that there will be some 'usual suspects'. Working through the Win Themes exercise, but putting yourself in the position of each main competitor can give an interesting and useful insight into how they may approach the rebid (or bid as it will be from their perspective). Putting all of the Win Themes from all of the competitors that you review can also give a sense of how truly unique some of your own Win Themes may, or may not, be.

Chapter 9 Checklist:

- Conduct a Green Field review of the contract and create a solution from the ground up.

- Generate a set of Win Themes and review them objectively.

- Start to put in place what changes you can to the contract delivery that anticipate changes the customer will be asking for to demonstrate your capability.

10

Pulling It All Together

Through the previous chapters we have covered a wide range of activities aimed at improving the likelihood of you as the incumbent successfully retaining your contract. The aim of this chapter is to pull all of these together and briefly summarize them to help show the complete 'set' of activities, and also to add some dos and don'ts at the final writing, pricing and presentation stage of the rebid competition that will help avoid some of the common pitfalls that even the most prepared incumbent rebid team can encounter.

The process of preparing your contract for a successful rebid started even before it was originally won at the initial bid stage. Depending on where you are in the contract and rebid cycle when reading this book you may or may not have the benefit of this full period of preparation and the background information about the contract from its very beginning. If you are close to the rebid period then you will potentially have lost a significant amount of the benefits that you would have had. You may struggle to capture early information from the contract period, and you may be in a position where the contract has not delivered a number of the things that are covered in previous chapters. However, all is not lost in gaining some advantage in the rebid and included below is a section on helping to pull back as much advantage as possible even if you have a limited time before the rebid process begins.

Summarizing the Full Process

Assuming that thinking about the rebid started at the very beginning of the contract then you will have to hand the following information and benefits covered in each of the preceding chapters. The first six chapters covered the work that will have been done from the start of the contract to build the strongest position possible for the rebid:

From Chapter 1 you will have:

- **A rebid file** that contains all the information from the very beginning of the contract period that will help you with the rebid, including for instance: a history of performance from the beginning of the contract (and performance of the activities before you started the contract); all the continuous improvement and added value initiatives that have been put in place over the contract period; reviews with the customer of the contract at regular intervals, including any positive comments and quotes from the customer; a history of any changes to the needs and circumstances of the customer and how the contract management team have reacted to help the customer in these changing situations and circumstances; a clear understanding of key players in the customer organization, their influence on the rebid and opinions on you as an incumbent.

- **Information from before you took over the contract** of performance levels that were being delivered to show how you have improved delivery over the contract period.

- **A promises register** that shows all the things that you promised to deliver in your original bid, together with when and how you actually delivered each of these promises during the initial implementation of the contract and beyond.

- **A record of your successful implementation** showing your proven ability to deliver a successful change programme on this contract with this customer.

- **A Contract Plan** that was started at the beginning of the contract and set out the strategy for the contract over its length and the changes that were planned for the contract over this period. This plan will have been implemented, reviewed regularly and updated as required. It will form a significant record of the successes you as incumbent have had in delivering changes and improvements for the customer on the contract over its period.

- **A performance measurement regime** set up at the start of the contract that records the initial performance of the contract in key areas.

From Chapter 2 you will have:

- A comprehensive record of key **performance measures** through the whole contract and how delivery against these has improved over the contract period.

- A record of how your performance **benchmarks** against other contracts or providers.

- A history of **customer responses** to improved performance.

- A record of how performance has had a positive **impact on the customer's own business**.

- How you have **added new performance** measures, with the customer, to record improvement in areas that have increased in importance over the period of the contract.

From Chapter 3 you will have:

- A complete record of the **added value** that has been delivered to the customer, including 'ad hoc' one-off added value incidents and a programme of planned added value initiatives.

- **A record** of how this added value has had a **positive impact on the customer**, including case studies of how your contract team reacted to issues, incidents or problems that the customer encountered and how you reacted to help.

- **Regular reviews** of the added value delivered.

- Costs to you (i.e. the **investment** your company has made) of these added value initiatives.

- A comprehensive programme of **continuous improvement** that has been delivered to the customer, including an analysis of the customer's most important needs.

- A record of how this improvement has **helped the customer.**

- **A comparison of performance** at the start of the contract compared to performance through and at the end of the contract – or as the rebid approaches, as evidence of how you will further improve over the next contract period.

- **A proven set of processes**, that the customer has bought into, that deliver this improvement.

From Chapter 4 you will have:

- A comprehensive **register of all the risks** that are relevant to the contract, and how these may have changed over the years.

- A full set of **mitigation actions** that you have taken to reduce the likelihood of these risks, and their impact should they occur.

- A complete **history of any events** that have occurred on the contract, how these came about, what your management team did to overcome them at the time and how well these actions worked.

- A clear history of how, through **learning from these events**, your company has updated its processes and systems on the contract to reduce the likelihood of them happening again.

- All of the above done with the customer and the **customer responses** to your plans and actions.

- A knowledge of how your company will be able to reduce the risks involved in the changes to the next contract period, and conversely the **risks that the customer would face in bringing in a new contractor** who does not know the contract so well.

From Chapter 5 you will have:

- A record of how the customers environment, organization and **needs have changed** over the period of the contract.

- A record of how your business has changed what and how it delivers on the contract to **match these changes** and meet emerging customer needs.

- A view of **where the customer is heading** in the future and what the likely changes are in their needs and how they will format the coming contract.

From Chapter 6 you will have:

- A full record of **all the customer's key decision makers**, influencers and other players who have been involved in the contract or may be involved in the rebid.

- An **understanding of their needs**, preferences and the things that are important to them.

- A map **of their own relationships** with each other and what they think of you and your performance on the contract.

- A strong and **positive set of relationships** with these key players.

Chapters 7, 8 and 9 will give you a head start in the rebid itself.

From Chapter 7 you will have:

- A full **rebid timetable** of actions the customer is taking for the rebid and when you are expected to have your own preparations completed by.

- Had some **influence** on what will go into the rebid and the next contract's format.

- **The right team** in place in good time for running and delivering the rebid.

From Chapter 8 you will have:

- An understanding of **what the customer is looking for** in the next contract period.

- **A clear and timed strategy** for how you will be approaching the rebid and what you want to put into the rebid documentation and presentations.

From Chapter 9 you will have:

- **An outline solution** for the next contract period.

- That has been **built up from first principles (Green Field solution)** based on knowledge of future customer needs – not simply a pared down version of what you are presently delivering.

- That has been **tested with the customer** and challenged and reviewed internally.

- Work already completed, perhaps through new initiatives on the contract, to **evidence to the customer that you are able to meet the needs** that they have for the forthcoming contract period.

To gauge where you actually are as you approach an imminent rebid, go through the table below, ticking the level of information you have to hand:

Area	Level that you have		
	Totally	Some	None
Complete rebid file			
Pre-contract performance levels			
Promises register			
Record of implementation			
Contract plan			
Performance record from start of contract			
Full performance record throughout contract			
Benchmarked performance against other contracts			
Record of impact of performance on customer			
Record of added value throughout the contract period			
Record of the impact of added value on the customer			
Record of all investments in added value initiatives			
Record of continuous improvement throughout the contract			
Clear process for how Continuous improvement was delivered			
Record of how continuous improvement helped the customer			
Record of customer reaction to continuous improvement			
History of risk registers showing changes over the contract			
History of mitigation actions put in place to reduce risks and impacts			
History of events and issues on the contract			
History of how these were dealt with positively			
Record of learning from events and resulting actions			

Record of positive customer reactions to your actions and processes			
List of risks customer would face in using another supplier			
Comprehensive review of the customer's changing environment			
Clear record of how the contract has reacted to changes in needs			
Clear understanding of the customer's future strategy			
Understanding of all customer key decision makers in the rebid			
Understanding of their individual needs and aims			
Complete map of the relationships between customer key players			
Strong understanding of their views of your company			
Strong relationships with each customer key player			
Clear understanding of the rebid timetable			
Influenced the format of the rebid			
Have the right team in place for the rebid and dedicated to the task			
An outline solution for the next contract based on customer needs			
The solution is based on first principles and has been reviewed internally			
The solution has been tested with the customer			
Work has been put in place to demonstrate the new solution will work			

If you mainly ticked 'totally' on the above list then you are in a strong position to make the most of the work done over the contract period to win your rebid. If you ticked mainly 'none' or 'some' then, depending on how long you have before the competition for the rebid actually starts then you are at a disadvantage compared with where you could be. However, below are a number of things you can do to pull back some advantage.

Actions If You Are Not Fully Prepared

Assuming you have just been assigned to run the rebid for a contract, but find that there is little available information about the contract to date, or that there has been little preparation completed there are a few things you can do to pull back some advantage. They won't substitute fully for where you could be if the contract had been prepared through its life, but they should give you some benefit when the rebid process starts. Obviously the more time you have before the bid documentation is published and the competition starts in earnest the better.

1. Ensure you have a team capable of delivering the rebid. You may need to bring in others from outside the contract, but you are also likely to need people from within the contract who have an understanding of how it works and the various relationships with

the customer. The team will need to be bought together as early as possible and, whilst there may be tensions between people bought in and those who have full time jobs on the contract, who also perhaps have little experience of rebidding and a sense that only minor changes will ensure a win, the team needs to quickly gain a sense of urgency and clarity of the task ahead.

2.   Assess the current position of the contract. Again you will need to look to a number of sources from outside and within the contract. Some of the areas to understand will include:

a) How well is the contract performing against the measures set down by the customer?

b) What is the state of the relationship with customer contacts, and their view of your company's performance to date? (You will perhaps need to cross reference responses from different parties – you may get very different views from different sources.)

c) What is the history of the contract – has performance been solid or variable, have there been issues during the contract period, have changes been made during the contract?

3.   Get as much information of the customer's intentions for the rebid as possible:

a) What is the timetable they are following and what are the key timings for the rebid?

b) What changes are they looking to make to the contract – are these minor or significant? The level and accuracy of information here will be dependent on the relationships that are already there between the customer and individuals within your business, however you may be able to glean some information from the next actions.

4.   Do a quick review of the customer and their environment:

a) What is happening in the customer's marketplace or sector – are there drivers that will impact on the customer, such as a need for cost reductions, or new ways of working that may impact on their plans.

b) How is the customer fairing? Are they growing, in trouble, changing strategy, etc. You will probably be able to get some of this information through a secondary search of information such as industry magazines, customer annual reports, press releases or stories from or about the customer. Having this external view will enable you to check any views you get from contacts within the customer or from those on your contract.

c) Has the customer run any bids or rebids recently in other areas? Finding information on these may give you a view of the sort of process the customer is likely to run, if they consistently use consultants to help run the process (and who these are). If you can obtain copies of the ITT/PQQ/RFPs they have produced as part of the process then you may get insight into the types of questions they may be asking and what is important to them. Understanding who won these contracts and why will give further ideas and insights.

5. Gather what information you can about the performance of the contract to date. This may be available from pulling together what you can find on the contract about the history of delivery, or may be through contract reports to the business. Try to pull together as much information from the contract history as possible and patch this together to give a timeline of performance.

6. Establish which organizations are likely to be competing against you for the contract, their strengths and weaknesses, contacts with the customer, how your company stacks up against them in key areas and what the bidding record of each of these competitors is.

Once you have this basic information together you should run a workshop with your rebid team and key managers from the contract. The aim is to review the information you have, gain any further information, and to ensure that all involved have a clear understanding of what will happen during the rebid. Key items on the agenda for this meeting will be:

- Confirm the rebid timetable and actions that will be required of the rebid team and the contract team at each stage.

- Establish the key customer players who will be involved at each stage of the bid. Establish an outline customer relationship map and identify who within the contract and rebid team should be key points of contact with each customer contact. You may also at this point be in a position to start identifying what information you wish to get via these relationships from different customer contacts – and what messages you may want to be putting out into the customer organization via these contacts.

- An improved understanding of the contract history, key events, changes that have occurred, added value delivered and performance levels (get documentary evidence if at all possible).

- Brainstorm the key needs the customer will have for the coming contract and what changes they will wish to see in the new contract.

- Run through an initial Strengths, Weaknesses, Opportunities and Threats for your company in the rebid vs. what you know about the customer's needs and the likely changes.

- Set out a plan of action for the rest of the rebid process and gain agreement from those within the contract to action what is required.

All of the above actions will need to be taken as quickly as possible so that you have as clear a picture as possible of the situation, can set up an action plan for the rebid and begin to set out your rebid strategy and outline solution for the new contract.

WHAT ABOUT AN EXTENSION TO THE EXISTING CONTRACT PERIOD?

Many contracts have the potential for extensions beyond the initial contract. Particularly in the public sector these will have been defined when the contract was initially publicized. The customer has no obligation to use these extension periods, but it may be in their interests to use them. It is usually in your interests as the incumbent to ask for the full length of extension possible as this means your guaranteed income from the contract is extended – and particularly so if you feel you are unprepared for the rebid. However it is worth thinking through some of the issues below before automatically asking for an extension from the customer:

- There may be benefits for the customer in extending the existing contract. Procurement processes cost money, and there are risks involved in bringing in new suppliers to balance against the potential for changes and cost reductions to be gained from the competitive process. Look at the customer's situation and work through the positives and negatives for them of an extension vs. a rebid now. Some customers are not themselves prepared fully for a rebid procurement. If they are not then you may use this to offer an extension to help them prepare. The customer may be going through a period of intensive change – think about how you could make changes over the coming period in the contract to help them during this period and offer these changes as part of an extension so that they can postpone the rebid until the changes are complete.

- Will changes to the contract or a price reduction act as an incentive to the customer to extend – and are these attractive to you as the supplier? If you are on extremely thin margins this may not be attractive to you. But if you are making high margins due to changes in the contract over the period and will have to reduce these as part of the rebid in order to be competitive, giving some of this profit away for an extension may be commercially sound. Not only will it extend the income from the contract, but it may act to smooth the reduction in price to the customer so that competitors prices at the rebid do not look significantly cheaper than you have been charging – with the potential dissonance this may cause the customer in their impression of how they may feel you have been exploiting them over the previous contract period with high prices and margins at their expense. If there are also changes to how the contract could be run that you have been prevented from putting in place, but which would be a good opportunity to test with the customer in preparation for the next contract period then a negotiation around an extension may be a good way for you to introduce these changes and show the customer that you can be innovative – and provide the chance for you to get back some of the investment in introducing these innovations from contract payments during the extension so that you can offer them at less cost to the customer in the next contract price.

- How would an extension make life easier for you or the competition due to the revised timing of the rebid? If a year extension to the contract means that the rebid coincides with several other rebids for you will you have the resources to rebid this contract properly? What about key competitors and their rebid/bid situations (as far as you can get this information)? Are key competitors close to introducing and proving new technology, innovations or acquisitions that may put them into a stronger position in a year's time and put your chances of winning at risk? Or would an extension either wrong foot your competitors – or conversely give them or you more time to prepare a better bid? Thinking through these pros and cons should be part of your thinking.

A decent period of extension to the contract will normally be a good thing, but always think through all the factors above, and also think carefully about how to approach the customer. You need to do so early and ensure that you put the request in terms that gives them an incentive to give the extension.

Some Do's and Don'ts for the Rebid

As the rebid goes into the final stages of completing bidding documents and delivering presentations all the skills of running a bid come into play. There are many books and training courses on bidding and I will not try to repeat or summarize them in this book. However, there are a number of issues particular to a rebid for an incumbent that it is worth finishing off this section, and book, by covering.

ENSURE THE RIGHT RELATIONSHIP BETWEEN THE REBID TEAM AND THE CONTRACT TEAM

Chapter 7 includes a section on who the rebid team could be made up from. For a rebid the situation is slightly different to a new bid in that there is a team of people available already running the contract and who should have a strong insight into the details of the customer and workings of the present solution. Even if a rebid team comprises people from outside the contract, key people from the contract will provide essential detailed information and customer relationships.

However the contract team can have quite a different perspective on the rebid and what is required in the solution to a team coming in from outside the contract. Sometimes the contract team is nervous about the impending competition – after all it is their jobs that will change most if the rebid is lost to a competitor. However, the contract team can also find themselves in a position where a rebid team from outside the contract is asking pointed questions about issues the contract may have had, why the contract is run the way it is, and proposing (through a Green Field Solution – see Chapter 9) significantly different ways that the new contract should be run, jobs perhaps reduced, and management organizations changed. This can be difficult for those involved from the contract team who feel they know the contract best (better than the new rebid team) and have been running it well for the past period. Some of the ideas and questions from the rebid team can appear naive or overly challenging to the contract team.

From the other perspective a rebid team coming in from outside the contract can feel that the contract team appear overly defensive of their performance to date. The contract team may seem to feel that the contract will be won by 'more of the same' and will come up with many reasons why it is difficult or impossible, and not necessary, to make changes to the contract (particularly cuts) in order to win the rebid. The rebid team may find that they are isolated from the customer contacts by the contract team's own relationships with these contacts and they are reluctant to help the rebid team build their own relationships with important players within the customer team. It may also be difficult for the rebid team to be too open with members of the contract team if the solution that the rebid team is thinking of takes these members of the contract team's jobs away – or may require someone with different skills or experience in the job to those of the present incumbent.

Ensuring that these tensions are recognized and resolved early is important to a successful rebid effort. Including a core team from the contract in the wider rebid team early will help, bearing in mind that the contract must still be run well and deliver, especially during the critical months prior to the rebid. This team will need to be communicated with early and perhaps even be seconded for short periods to other rebids to give them a view of the process from a more objective viewpoint, prior to the more subjective involvement in their own contract's rebid. Creating a shared purpose for the full rebid team (i.e. winning) and acknowledging that the tensions above may occur can also give the team a sense of perspective and understanding of the task in hand.

DON'T ASSUME THAT YOU WILL AUTOMATICALLY PRE-QUALIFY FOR THE REBID

Particularly in the public sector there is usually an initial bid stage of pre-qualification where the tender is put out to the market and bidders invited to put in to the customer their qualifications for running the contract. From these pre-qualification bids a short list of potential suppliers is chosen to go to the next stage.

There is a real danger of complacency from the incumbent at this stage and there are many examples of incumbents not pre-qualifying from the early stages of their own rebid. Take the pre-qualification process seriously and ensure that you put your best effort into the forms. Some rebidders have been known to miss out because they assume the customer knows what the company is already delivering on the contract and don't include the sort of strong, thought through arguments, references and examples from their existing contract that they would if they were bidding for the first time and using other contract examples. Because pre-qualification documents and evaluations are often relatively mechanistic, with pass/fail criteria, basic information on the business etc., they are usually marked mechanistically. Even if the evaluator knows what you are delivering on the contract if the information is not written in the pre-qualification submission they cannot give marks for it.

Equally if you also have other contracts delivering similar work to what is required in the new contract include information from these. You do not want to give the customer the impression that this contract is the only experience that you have, so don't lean entirely on your experience of this contract. This will especially be the case if the customer is changing the form of the next contract, either in the breadth of services required, how they are delivered, in the pricing mechanism or any other significant way. You need to show that you have detailed knowledge of the customer and their needs and a history of delivery on this contract, but not that you are only able to deliver more of the same. Your competitors will be looking to show how they can deliver the contract well and in innovative ways – don't let the customer get the impression that you are not also able to deliver new thinking and innovation for the coming contract period.

Your aim for the pre-qualification should not just be to fill in the questionnaire, but to get the maximum possible marks and impress the customer putting your company in the lead at an early stage of the process.

USING QUESTIONS IN THE BID PROCESS

As the incumbent you should know considerably more detail about the existing contract than your competitors. Included in this will be the full extent of the work and costs required to deliver the contract. Many bid processes allow bidders to ask official questions of the customer during the process. Usually, especially in public sector contracts, the customer will publish these questions and their answer to all competitors bidding. Normally the incumbent will not wish to reveal additional information to competitors through asking questions in this way. However, there are circumstances where you can use questions to help your cause.

One of the potential dangers from competitors who do not know the contract is that they exclude certain costs in their solution and therefore their price and potentially win the contract, but then find they have to bear the additional costs they were unaware of. But you have still lost the contract.

If there are costs or activities that you are aware of that the customer has not made clear in the bid documents then asking an official question about these costs or activities can ensure that they are revealed to your competitors so they are taken into account. Ideally, you will have used your relationship with the customer to ensure that during their preparations for the procurements they are aware of and have included key cost areas in the bid documentation. Some of these will be required by legislation in many countries – such as staff numbers and costs for Transfer of Undertaking and Protection of Employment (TUPE) information in the UK. However, there can often be cases where the final procurement documentation sent to all bidders does not include a description of elements that will form part of the costs of the contract.

There is an alternative route that you can take: by not revealing these costs and using your knowledge of the contract in your submission to talk in detail about the activities and clearly pointing out that if others have not taken into account these activities in their solution and price then their bid will be incomplete – but this is a very risky approach for a number of reasons:

- Customer evaluation processes may evaluate price and quality separately and so not connect what you point out in your written submission with your price – so your argument regarding why you have added cost in for activities not covered by other bidders may be lost.

- The customer may feel that you are attempting to increase the costs of the contract unnecessarily and again discount your argument.

- Customers under cost pressures may decide to take the lower price and give the challenge to the winning competitor to deliver for their quoted price anyway.

- Particularly in the public sector, customers are strongly challenged by senior managers, politicians or auditors to choose the 'best value' bid. If this is not the lowest price bid then this challenge is significantly greater and so customers may choose to take the lowest price contract and worry about the delivery aspects later.

The more successful approach is usually to ensure that competitors are aware of all the costs of the contract and therefore (hopefully) factor these into their price.

Obviously you will only want to reveal the sort of information that is likely to increase the price of your competitors bids to cover all relevant aspects of the contract, whilst not giving away information that you as the incumbent can use to show your own in-depth knowledge of the contract and the superiority of the solution you are delivering for the coming contract period. Finding this balance will depend on the specifics of your contract, customer and rebid strategy.

A related issue can emerge if your rebid is being conducted by the customer through what is increasingly known as a 'Competitive Dialogue' approach, where the customer holds a series of meetings with each bidder to discuss and challenge different aspects of their solutions. This is an intensive process for the customer procurement team, but one that is intended to ensure that final bids are all stronger as bidders have been able to get some feedback from the customer on their solution. It can also mean that the customer challenges bidders to show innovative approaches and solutions during this dialogue phase enabling the customer to modify their specification for the bid to reflect the best possible solutions. For bidders, however, it can inevitably mean that some of their best ideas and innovations get taken up by the customer in their revised specifications and in effect 'given away' to the competition.

As the incumbent you need to find the right balance during the Competitive Dialogue phase between giving away too much information that will be of crucial benefit to your competitors and appearing not to be innovative to your customer. On the positive side this phase can be an opportunity to show the customer that you are not just a 'safe pair of hands' – particularly if the customer is focusing on changes in the contract and is looking for new approaches. Using Competitive Dialogue to introduce new ideas to the customer (or ideally ideas that you have been testing with the customer for the previous few months) and showing how they would be used fully in the new contract can help reinforce your position as the supplier that is forward thinking from a strong base of knowledge of the contract. Be careful, however, of dismissing the ideas of other competitors as unworkable. This could lead the customer to seeing you as being reactive and stuck in your ways as a supplier. If the ideas are good take them on and add your knowledge of the contract to show how you would make them work with the lowest risk of change. If the ideas are genuinely unworkable be sure to show the customer in detailed and objective ways why, and ideally show how the benefits or principles of the idea could be delivered differently.

PRICE THE CUSTOMER'S SPECIFICATION, NOT WHAT YOU KNOW

Whilst knowing the details of how a contract you are rebidding runs and the costs involved is a big advantage to you as the incumbent, it can also be a danger. In the rebid documents the customer will have specified what they want for the coming period and your competitors will cost this and price accordingly. Whilst on occasion this can mean that their bid is seen as non-compliant, or too cheap to be realistic, much more often the customer will take the lower priced bid. I have seen a number of incumbents make the mistake of pricing higher than the competition because they have added in a range of costs that they know the contract requires but were not clearly set out in the customer's documentation – and losing the rebid. Despite protestations after the announcement that the competition has not fully priced the contract the customer rarely reverses their decision; and knowing that the winner will have to take on these costs is cold comfort for the losing incumbent. You should have had plenty of opportunities to ensure that the customer is aware of the full costs of delivering the contract and that these are included in the rebid documentation prior to the bid documentation being released through your relationship with the customer, or through questions during the rebid process as covered above. You should also have taken the opportunity to create a Green Field solution (see Chapter 9) that will have taken a ground up approach to the contract and hopefully avoided any assumptions built up over the contract period. The final route to ensuring a competitive solution is to check every aspect of your solution and costing against the specification the customer has given for the rebid. Look at every cost item and aspect of the solution you are proposing and make sure you are clear which part of the specification it delivers to. Then check if you could meet the specification without this aspect of your solution – or if you can find a way to deliver it at a lower cost. Look at every idea, every bit of added value that you are delivering and compare the value it adds with the cost it adds. Ensure that if you do add in costs that they are fully justified to the customer in your written submission with the strong benefits they deliver. Or if the customer is looking primarily at reducing the price of the contract then look very seriously at taking them out of your solution.

If you find yourself in the position that you have key parts of your solution that you need in the bid to make the contract viable, but which have not been added to the customers specification and so might not be added to competitors bids and prices, then consider putting in an additional alternative solution beyond the compliant bid that sets out these costs and the essential nature of the activity they are based on to the delivery of the contract. The customer may not take on this alternative option, but it at least sets a pointer for later negotiations and sets out clearly the areas you see as essential whilst still enabling you to put in a competitive price in your core bid that meets the customer specification.

USING YOUR KNOWLEDGE TO KNOCK OUT ALTERNATIVES

Using your detailed knowledge of the contract in your rebid should not only be used to justify your own solution. It can also be used to cast doubt in the customer's mind about alternative solutions that your competitors may propose. A good way to structure this is to write out in your bid documentation a number of possible solutions that you have 'considered' for specific aspects of the work to be delivered and then give detailed and specific reasons (ideally with real life examples and case studies from the contract) why each of them apart from your own chosen solution would be inferior. This does add significantly to the length of your written solution or presentations, and must be carefully handled if the customer is restricting the number of words to be used or time in presentations, perhaps just focusing on one or two key parts of the solution, but it can be a powerful way to show the customer how you have used your experience to deliver the best solution – and put real doubts in their minds if competitors have offered one of your rejected alternatives without fully justifying them.

Be careful not to imply that the contract cannot be delivered in any way other than you are proposing – this would give the customer a sense that you are yourself blinded to alternatives. Rather point out the additional costs of, or issues that make alternative solutions inferior for the customer. Use specific examples that evidence your assertions from the contract (e.g. would an alternative solution work for specific customer groups, or at particularly busy periods that you can give figures for the level of demand over different time periods to prove, or work with a key customer process or piece of software etc.).

NEVER UNDERESTIMATE THE COMPETITION

It may seem strange to finish a book that aims to improve the incumbent's chances of winning the rebid to talk about the dangers of competition. An appreciation of the competition is an obvious part of bidding. But there are real dangers that incumbents face in terms of their attitudes to the competition that it are worth covering – and even the companies with the best records of rebidding (e.g. around 90 per cent retention) still lose some contracts at rebid. Whilst having a clear understanding of the contract is a big advantage, it can sometimes foster a feeling that the competition has little chance of taking the contract. With such a strong understanding of the customer, how the contract works and a record of delivery how can others without this knowledge successfully compete? However ignoring the options that competitors may put to the customer and not reacting to these appropriately is a gap in the approach of a rebid effort that can create a real danger.

The first action in looking at the competition is to review the likely set of competitors prior to the start of the rebid process. Most businesses have a regular set of competitors who bid against them with varying levels of success. Analyse these competitors, their approaches, their contact with the customer if known, and any contracts that they may have elsewhere of a similar nature to the contract being rebid. Build up a bidding scenario for each of these competitors looking at the contract from their perspective.

Some businesses run workshops with teams of people from across the business (some of whom may even previously have worked for the competitor if there is a degree of natural movement of staff across key competitors in an industry) who are asked to put themselves in the position of each competitor and put together a strategy of how they, as that competitor, would approach the bid. This will often involve a Strengths, Weaknesses, Opportunities and Threats (SWOT) analysis done from the competitor's viewpoint together with a Green Field approach using the known experiences, capabilities, etc. of the competitor and a view of what Win Themes the competitor will push in their bid. Of course these will only be guides to how the competitor may approach the bid and bring no guarantees of accuracy, but the results can be extremely useful for the rebid team (who should not dominate the workshop – some businesses even exclude them completely). The key is to focus on the mindset of the competitor and have the team involved really look at the situation with the view of winning it from the competitor's viewpoint. Too often if rebid teams attempt such an exercise themselves their thinking is dominated by their own company viewpoint and too many negative assumptions about the competitor and their chances are bought into the process. The resulting bid strategies for each main competitor should then be addressed seriously by the rebid team and the rebid strategy reviewed to ensure that threats from competitors are taken into account. As the rebid process progresses it is likely that other competitors will be longlisted or even shortlisted by the customer to compete for the contract. Don't ignore these competitors even if they are new to you. They will, if they have succeeded in getting onto the customer's list of potential suppliers, have been able to put forward credentials that the customer is taking seriously. A number of rebids have been lost to competitors that the incumbent team have dismissed as too small, too inexperienced, or too new to the industry to possibly win the contract and have not been properly reviewed by the rebid team and their potential strengths and approaches have not therefore been taken into proper account. Repeat the above exercise for these competitors, having undertaken research on them – their strengths and experiences even if they are from other industry areas, their potential approaches, and how they might bring in new thinking, capabilities and assets that they could leverage to save the customer money, deliver in a different way, or offer added value that the 'usual suspect' competitors in your industry do not presently offer. Look at the potential wider strategy of these new competitors:

- Are they looking for a foothold in this industry and this contract will be the start of a market entry strategy and so a key target for them?

- Do they have significant financial backing that will allow them to invest in the contract? Do they work in significantly lower margin industries and so will bid at a lower margin that the accepted norm in your industry?

- Do they have experience in other regions or countries that they may be bringing into your region?

- Do they have experience in related fields that they are looking to expand and through which they can bring experience and cost savings to the customer?

- Have they recently been acquired (or made an acquisition) that brings fresh capability?

Ensuring that you properly review your competitors and take seriously their potential to win the contract will help you overcome the threat they pose. Your challenge is to balance this awareness with a clear focus on the customer and how you will deliver a solution that best meets their needs.

Finally

Using the techniques and ideas in this book will give you a significantly better chance of winning your rebid. There is of course never certainty in bidding and even the best prepared and experienced companies occasionally lose. But the odds of retaining your contract will – through thorough preparation, a real focus on what the customer wants and expects, and not having an attitude that you have the right to continue to deliver the contract as you have to date – be greatly increased. And once you have won your rebid be sure to start the new contract period with the next rebid in mind, so that you can continue and build your relationship with the customer for well into the future.

Chapter 10 Checklist:

- If not fully prepared follow the actions given.

- Think about the possibility of an extension to the contract.

- Ensure there is the right relationship between rebid team and contract team.

- Don't assume that you will pre-qualify for the rebid.

- Look at how you can best use questions in the rebid process.

- Price the customer's specification, not what you know of the contract.

- Knock out other solutions by showing why your solution is the best and others will not work.

- Never underestimate the competition.

Index

Locators shown in *italics* refer to figures and tables.

action, customer need
importance for retaining contract
relevance, 76–8, *76, 77*
anticipation, customer need
importance for retaining contract
relevance, 72–5
assessment, outcome
need for as element of rebid
strategy, 114–15
assumptions
need for control of in rebid process,
140–41

benchmarks and benchmarking
importance as element of contract
performance measurement,
35–8, 129
benefits, one-off
characteristics as element of added
value, 50–51
budgets, rebid
need for as element of rebid
strategy plans, 115
businesses
case study of contract performance
measurement, 34–5

capabilities, customer need
importance for retaining contract
relevance, 76–8, *76, 77*
case studies
changing markets and customer
need, 81–7
contract performance measurement,
34–5
incumbent-customer relationships,
95–9, *98*
possible pathways of contract
performance measurement,
40–42
use of benchmarking, 36–8
centres, shared service
appropriateness of as rebidding
risk consideration, 61
change
anticipating and acting on customer
need, 72–8, *76, 77*
importance of potential
performance at rebid, 31–2
need for as element of rebid
strategy plans, 115
need for provision of lowest risk
in rebidding, 59–63, *60*

type and consequences of customer
risk, 57
see also management, solution and
change
closure, need for
impact on contract need, 72
collation, risks
role in management of bidding
process, 63–6, *63*, *65*
commitments, customer
salience of record keeping of,
17–18, *18*
communication and communicating
importance of added value and
continuous assessment, 48–9
salience of provider-customer at
contract start, 16–17
companies, incumbent
benefits held at rebid, 2–4
implications of rebid losses, 4–5
involvement in rebid preparation,
105–11, *106*
salience of communication of at
contract start, 16–17
see also relationships, incumbent-
customer
see also factors affecting e.g.
improvement, continuous;
value, added
competition, rebidding
need to avoid under-estimation
of, 145–7
compilation, mid-term review
salience, purpose and process, 90–91
computers
appropriateness of as rebidding
risk consideration, 61
impact on contract changing
needs, 71–2
contracts

director's note on investment in
existing, 86–7
elements that change nature and
content of, 70–72
overview of rebid planning
involving, 8–10
see also delivery, contract;
extensions, contract;
implementation, contract;
plans, contract; profitability,
contract; relevance, contract;
teams, rebid and contract
see also aspects for consideration e.g.
improvement, continuous;
value, added
see also tools enabling successful
e.g. files, rebid; information,
performance and customers;
knowledge, contract;
measurement, performance
corporate social responsibility (CSR)
as source of added value, 52
costs, contract
impact of added value on, 53–4
culture, customer
compatibility of as incumbent
benefit at rebid, 3–4
customers
case study of changing markets
and needs of, 81–7
information of as source of added
value, 52
responses and consequences of
risk management, 57–9, *58*
salience of communication of at
start of contract, 16–17
stages of rebidding process from
perspective of 105–8, *106*
understanding of as incumbent
benefit at rebid, 2

see also need, customer;
relationships, incumbent-
customer

delivery, contract
proof of as incumbent benefit at
rebid, 2–3
role of risk registers and logs, 63–6,
63, 65
see also influences e.g. need, customer
documents *see* records

efficiency
incumbent possession of as benefit
at rebid, 3
equipment, provision of
appropriateness of as rebidding
risk consideration, 61
evaluation, performance *see*
measurement, performance
events, logs of
role in recording risks, 65–6
experience, manager
appropriateness of as rebidding
risk consideration, 61
extensions, contract
characteristics and benefits, 136–8

failure
need for provision of lowest risk
in rebidding, 59–63, *60*
files, rebid
characteristics, 128
salience of creating at start of
contract, 14–15

Green Field Review
characteristics and role in rebid
solution, 118–21

handovers, project

timing of as consideration in
rebidding risk management, 62

implementation, contract
importance of maintaining record
of, 18–19, 128
improvement, continuous
actions to achieve, 32–5, *32, 33*
definition, characteristics and
purpose, 46–9
importance of ability to ensure
among incumbents, 31
overcoming barriers to, 48–9
utilisation in rebid process, 55–6
incumbents *see* companies,
incumbent
indicators, key performance, 2–3
industries, supply
director's note on best practice in,
85–6
information, performance and
customer
appropriateness of as rebidding
risk consideration, 61
as source of added value, 52
gathering of as element of rebid
team preparation, 110
importance of using existing
effectively, 26–7
purpose and process of collation
for mid-term review, 90–91
salience of capturing at start of
contract, 13–14, 128
information technology
appropriateness of as rebidding
risk consideration, 61
impact on contract changing
needs, 71–2
initiatives, work
characteristics and possible added
value, 51–3

inputs
    as element of contract performance
        measurement, 28–35
investment
    as source of added value, 52
    director's note on existing contracts
        and, 86–7
invitation to tender (ITT), 73
invoices and invoicing
    as source of added value, 52

Job Training Partnership Act (USA,
        1982), 40

key performance indicators, 2–3
knowledge, contract
    importance in rebidding process,
        144–5

logs, event
    role in recording risks, 65–6

management, risk
    customer responses and factors
        influencing, 57–9, 58
    suggestions for rebid preparation,
        59–63, 60
    see also tools e.g. registers, risk
management, solution and change
    gathering of as element of rebid
        team preparation, 110
mapping, relationship
    salience and process, 95–9, 98
markets, best practice
    importance of adhering to retain
        contract relevance, 78–9
measurement, performance
    case study of, 34–5
    characteristics and salience of
        collating contract, 27–35

importance of contract, 35–8
importance of inputs, outputs and
    outcomes as element of contract,
    28–35
possible future pathways in
    contract, 40–42
salience at start of contract, 15–16,
    128, 129
uses of contract, 39–40
see also elements collated
    e.g. benchmarks and
    benchmarking
measurement, rebid
    importance of ensuring successful,
        26–7
mid-term reviews
    purpose and process, 87–92

need, customer
    anticipating and acting on changes
        in, 72–8, 76, 77
    case study of changing markets
        and, 81–7
    director's note on changing, 84–5
    salience of changing to retain
        contract relevance, 70–72
New Deal initiative (UK), 40
notes, director
    best practice in supply industry,
        85–6
    changing customer needs, 84–5
    investment in existing contracts,
        86–7
    overview of contract rebid
        planning, 8–10, 9
    starting contracts with end in
        mind, 22–3
objectives, winning
    strengths and weaknesses in rebid

solution preparation, 121–5,
    123, 124
Office of Government Commerce, 35,
    107
offices, provision of
    appropriateness as rebidding risk
        consideration, 61
outcomes and outputs
    as element of contract performance
        measurement, 28–35
    assessment of as element of rebid
        strategy, 114–15
    impact on contract changing
        needs, 71
    plans of as element of rebid
        strategy, 115–16
overlap, project
    timing of as consideration in
        rebidding risk management, 62

partnerships, incumbent-customer
    see relationships, incumbent-
        customer
Payment by Results (PbR), 40–41
performance
    actions to achieve incumbent,
        32–5, 32, 33
    characteristics and salience of
        collating contract, 27–35
    customer responses to improved,
        129
    importance of ensuring evaluation
        in bidding, 26–7
    improving levels of contract, 38–9
    information of as source of added
        value, 52
    salience of information of at start
        of contract, 13–14, 128
    see also measurement,
        performance

planned added value
    characteristics and possible
        initiatives, 51–3
plans, contract
    characteristics and importance of
        initial, 19–22, 128
    overview of rebid, 8–10
    salience of added value and
        continuous improvement, 46–7
    see also influences e.g. need, customer
plans, outcome and work
    need for as element of rebid
        strategy, 115–16
practice, best
    director's note on supply
        industry, 85–6
    importance of adhering to retain
        market contract relevance,
        78–9
pre-qualification questionnaires
    (PQQs), 73
presentation, mid-term review
    salience, purpose and process, 91–2
prices
    importance in rebidding process,
        143–4
    need for as element of rebid
        strategy plans, 115
procedures, work
    appropriateness of as rebidding
        risk consideration, 61
    need for as element of rebid
        strategy, 116
procurement, services
    changing patterns of, 82–3
profitability, contract
    impact of added value on, 53–4
programmes, work
    need for as element of rebid
        strategy, 116

projects
    overlap and handover of as element
        of rebidding risk management,
        62
promises, customer
    salience of keeping records of,
        17–18, *18*
providers, contract
    salience of communication of at
        start of contract, 16–17

questions
    appropriateness and use in rebid
        process, 141–3

rebids and rebidding
    dos and don'ts for process of,
        138–47
    examples of actions when not
        fully prepared, 133–8
    examples of simplified statements
        of, *60*
    implications of loss for incumbent
        company, 4–5
    importance of contract relevance
        at rebid, 69–70
    incumbent benefits at time of, 2–4
    stages of from customer
        perspective, 105–8, *106*
    summary of process and
        outcomes, 127–33, *132, 133*
    utilisation of added value and
        continuous improvement, 55–6
    see also solutions; strategies, rebid
    see also elements and influences e.g.
        contracts; failure; files, rebid;
        information, performance and
        customer; measurement, rebid;
        risk; teams, rebid and contract;
        training, staff

records
    importance of maintenance of
        customer promise, 17–18, *18*
    of performance, 129
    of successful implementation, 128
    role of risk in management of
        bidding process, 63–6, *63, 65*
    salience of maintaining contract
        implementation, 18–19
    using performance measures
        within rebid, 39–40
    see also communication; information,
        performance and customer
    see also types e.g. contracts; registers;
        reports and reporting; reviews
reduction, risk
    customer responses and factors
        influencing, 57–9, *58*
    suggestions for rebid preparation,
        59–63, *60*
    see also tools e.g. registers, risk
registers
    characteristics of promise, 120
    importance of maintenance of
        promise, 17–18, *18*
    role of risk in management of
        bidding process, 63–6, *63, 65*
relationships, incumbent-customer
    importance as element of rebid
        strategy, 115–16
    importance in contract
        performance measurement, 31
    importance to ensure contract
        relevance, 79–81
    prerequisites, building and
        managing of, 93–9, *98*
    responsibility for managing, 99–101
relevance, contract
    importance at time of rebid, 69–70
    importance of best practice to
        ensure, 78–9

importance of incumbent-
customer relationships, 79–81
see also influences e.g. need, customer
reports and reporting
importance of added value in
rebidding process, 55–6
resources, work
need for as element of rebid
strategy plans, 115
responsibility, corporate social
as source of added value, 52
reviews
as element of rebid strategy, 113–14
importance of added value in
rebidding process, 55–6
need for as element of rebid
strategy plans, 115
see also type e.g. Green Field
Review; mid-term reviews
risk
factors influencing level and
customer response to, 57–8
reduction of as incumbent benefit
at rebid, 3
use as element of rebid process,
59–60, *60*
see also management, risk
see also tools e.g. registers, risk

service centres, shared
appropriateness of as rebidding
risk consideration, 61
services
changing patterns of
procurement, 82–3
social responsibility, corporate
as source of added value, 52
solutions
management of as element of
rebid preparation, 110

process of rebid preparation,
117–25, *123, 124*
statements, rebid
examples of simplified, *60*
stock, provision of
appropriateness of as rebidding
risk consideration, 61
strategies, rebid
elements and processes, 113–16
streams, work
need for as element of rebid
strategy, 116
suppliers
as source of added value, 52
type and consequences of change
of, 57
supply, industry of
director's note on best practice in,
85–6
systems, work
appropriateness of as rebidding
risk consideration, 61

tasks
impact on contract changing need,
71
understanding of as incumbent
benefit at rebid, 2
teams, rebid and contract
importance of relationship
between, 138–40
role and responsibilities, 108–11
technologies, new
appropriateness as rebidding risk
consideration, 61
impact on contract changing
needs, 71–2
timetables
need for as element of rebid
strategy plans, 115

rebidding process from customer
  perspective, 105–8, *106*
training, staff
  appropriateness of as rebidding
    risk consideration, 61

value, added
  costs and impact on contract
    profitability, 53–4
  definition and characteristics,
    45–6
  impact on contract plans, 46–7
  importance of to communication,
    48–9
  possible initiatives involving,
    51–3
  utilisation in rebid process, 55–6

see also elements e.g. benefits, one-
  off; planned added value

warehousing, provision of
  appropriateness of as rebidding
    risk consideration, 61
'win themes'
  strengths and weaknesses in rebid
    solution preparation, 121–5,
    123, 124
work, programmes of
  need for as element of rebid
    strategy, 116
Working Nation programme
  (Australia), 40
writing, mid-term review
  salience, purpose and process, 90–91